The CÉLORON EXPEDITION to the Ohio Country 1749

The Reports of
Pierre-Joseph Céloron
and Father Bonnecamps

Edited by *Andrew Gallup*

HERITAGE BOOKS
2008

HERITAGE BOOKS

AN IMPRINT OF HERITAGE BOOKS, INC.

Books, CDs, and more—Worldwide

For our listing of thousands of titles see our website
at
www.HeritageBooks.com

Published 2008 by
HERITAGE BOOKS, INC.
Publishing Division
100 Railroad Ave. #104
Westminster, Maryland 21157

Other books by the author:

A Sketch of the Virginia Soldier in the Revolution

La Marine: The French Colonial Soldier in Canada, 1745-1761
Andrew Gallup and Donald F. Shaffer

Memoir of a French and Indian War Soldier
"Jolicoeur" Charles Bonin

International Standard Book Numbers
Paperbound: 978-0-7884-0606-5
Clothbound: 978-0-7884-7289-3

In memory of Tim Cook and all those who have gone before

CONTENTS

MAPS

PREFACE

Few North Americans have heard of the 1749 French expedition into western Pennsylvania and southern Ohio. The limited interest in this trek, usually called the Celoron Expedition, has often centered on the lead plates that the French buried along the Allegheny River and Ohio River. Yet, is there a significance to the Celoron Expedition beyond that of antiquarian curiosity? Francis Parkman, the pioneer writer of French, English, Indian, colonial conflicts, devoted a chapter to the expedition in **Montcalm and Wolfe**. Later historians have given the event less space, although the extent of the various works must be considered. At the time, the expedition was probably newsworthy, but not a headline producer. It is, however, an identifiable point on the road of change in North American history. It was an important step toward what turned out to be the finale of the ongoing battle between France and England for dominance in the New World.

These reports of the expedition also have value as a snapshot of the state of the Ohio country during this important period. The British had effectively penetrated this region by their trade with the native inhabitants. They were impacting on the economic and security interests of New France. The French believed the English were trespassing on their land, their land because of claims by early French explorers. The English, of course, did not agree. They argued that the region was theirs because the Iroquois had conquered it in the previous century and they ruled the Iroquois. France had agreed to English dominance of the Iroquois in the 1713 Treaty of Utrecht. They did take exception, however, to the issue of Iroquois dominion over this territory, stating that France had claimed the land before the Iroquois had invaded. To both European powers it was neat and tidy. The Native Americans had another viewpoint. As usual, their claim was not recognized or understood by the white men.

The purpose of the Celoron expedition was to eliminate any confusion concerning ownership of the Ohio country. It is doubtful if Celoron believed this would be the result. It is likewise doubtful if the Governor-General of New France, La Galissonière, believed it. The Governor, an experienced senior officer in the navy, had been too long defending France to have any illusion as to whether the British would meekly agree to stay east of the mountains. Celoron, as commander of western posts, Detroit and Fort Niagara, had continually dealt with British traders as economic and political agents of British policy among the native populations. La Galissonière may have understood this as part of the grand game at court. Celoron may have understood the situation on another level, the brutality of politics in the forest. Yet, neither man would have thought this expedition was an end, although both probably saw it as necessary.

Where does the Celoron Expedition fit into the larger picture? If the British Indian traders had not entered into the Ohio country in great numbers, the expedition probably would not have been sent. Had the expedition not been sent, the English Ohio Company might not have pushed to have a fort constructed at the forks of the Ohio, at least not for a few more years. Then the French might not have fortified western Pennsylvania when they did, and Washington may not have made his debut as Virginia Governor Dinwiddie's ambassador to the French in 1752. This leads on and on and perhaps it is best to let the reader weigh the importance of events.

Regardless of the expedition's impact on history, the reports presented here are interesting and informative. It is remarkable that they are independent of one another. This is rare in primary documents of the period. Then, as now, there was pressure to follow the party line, often enough to produce identical words with different signatures. This is not to suggest they represent opposing factions. They do, however, represent different viewpoints. Two men, both in very disciplined professions, tell it as they saw it with little or no diplomatic propriety.

Finally, while these journals have not been inaccessible to historians, they have not been readily accessible. **The Ohio Archaeological and Historical Publications**, Volume XXIX (1920), from which these reports are taken, is available in many large libraries and occasionally in used-book stores. This edition will, perhaps, make research a bit more convenient. Also, the notes by Reverend A.A. Lambing in the earlier publication are dated. Those included here are entirely the responsibility of the present editor. The reader may wish to consult the original publication to see the debate of that time over various aspects of the expedition and journals. As with the notes, the maps (not to scale) are the work of the editor and are included to provide the reader with a simple geographical orientation.

The editor wishes to thank the Ohio Historical Society for their permission to reprint the Celeron Journal and Father Bonnecamps' report.

AG 1996

INTRODUCTION

On June 15, 1749, at about three o'clock in the afternoon, twenty-three canoes carrying two hundred forty seven men left La Chine (near Montreal). Their mission was to reestablish French dominion over the Ohio country, a region broadly defined as the land along and north of the Allegheny and Ohio Rivers to Lake Erie and west to the Wabash River, in present-day Indiana. Few, if any of the expedition members had been to this region. There is no evidence that the expedition's commander, Pierre-Joseph Celoron de Blainville, had first-hand knowledge of *La Belle Riviere*, as the French called the area.

The Canadian-born Celoron, however, had ample frontier experience. He began serving France in 1707, as a cadet in the colonial troops. Undoubtedly, he had many years of active service in the west before receiving his captaincy and becoming commandant of Fort Michilimackinac (Mackinaw City, Michigan) in 1738. The next two years he was a senior officer in the expedition against the Chickasaws, after which he was awarded the Cross of St. Louis. He subsequently served as commandant of Detroit (Michigan), Fort Niagara (Youngstown, New York), and Fort St. Frederic (Crown Point, New York) (Dictionary of Canadian Biography III. 1974:99-100).

In Quebec, the Indendant of Canada, Francois Bigot, wrote to France. "M. de Celoron's party, which has been to the Belle Riviere, is also going to cost a large amount" (Shortt II. 1925:789).Why did the government of New France, who would have to justify the cost to a skeptical ministry and King, send these men west? Why did they believe this expedition was necessary?

1

THE MARQUIS DE BEAUHARNOIS TO THE MINISTER

8th October, 1744

On receiving intelligence this spring of the different settlements and magazines the English have formed on the Beautiful River, I issued my orders and sent belts to the Detroit nations to drive them thence by force of arms and to plunder the stores they have there; I gave like orders to the Commandant among the Ouiatanons, and the Miamis. Therefore, according to what the Outaouacas and Pontouatamiss of Detroit have promised me this summer at Montreal, and what the Commandants of the other posts have written to me respecting the dispositions of the Indians, I have reason to presume that these will act against the English settled on the Beautiful River, and also against the other settlements the latter may possibly form in that vicinity, and which the former will not suffer, as, independent of the war that I have had chanted in all the villages, they have accepted the belts presented on that occasion (O'Callaghan IX. 1855:1105).

Beauharnois was a pragmatist and used any resource to achieve a desired goal. Using Indians to further French policy would be seen as unethical or immoral by most Europeans. The Governor, however, had prior experience, and no regrets, in using these allies. Notable among his earlier efforts was the near destruction of the Fox people near Green Bay, Wisconsin.

The Ohio River Valley and the Great Lakes region proved to be too politically complicated and had too many players to be dominated using surrogate forces. It was one thing to encourage a group to attack another group who had long been seen as a traditional enemy. It was another thing to expect allied Indians to attack representatives of a formidable enemy, the English, and risk retribution not only from the English, but also from the nations along the Ohio River who were dependent on Anglo-American traders. Goods from Great Britain were less expensive, and often of better quality than French. In the eighteenth century forests of North America there was a link between violence and economic issues.

Beauharnois' policy was less than successful. English traders remained well established in (present-day) southwestern Ohio.

RAYMOND TO THE FRENCH MINISTER.

Quebec, November 2, 1747.

MONSEIGNEUR, Your Grace has been informed that the hurons of detroit and the Yrocois at the outlet of la Rivière Blanche have killed some Frenchmen at Sandoské; that those same Savages and other nations had Planned Together to carry off father poitiers, the missionary of the hurons, and Monsieur the Chevalier de Longoeuil, the Commandant of detroit; to Make themselves masters of that fort and to slaughter the inhabitants: the plot of Those Savages was discovered and this fortunately caused its failure.

This leads me to take the liberty of Begging you, Monseigneur, to observe that I had predicted to you the Revolt and unfaithfulness of the Savages of the Country around detroit. As Your Grace must have Remarked in the memorial I Had the honor of Sending You from Niagara on this Subject In 1745, in which I took the liberty of Pointing out to you all the evil there was to Fear for the upper countries from the English Traders who were allowed to Establish themselves at la Rivière Blanche in the Vicinity of detroit and of the other posts; that the English would infallibly corrupt and Win over the Savage nations that live with Them on That River. And This has not failed to happen As I had predicted to you. They have succeeded so well in making them their devoted Creatures that it is these same Savages who at their instigation have killed the French at Sandoské; who Wished to Surprise detroit to put those same English there; who, As there is every reason to Believe, have borne their presents, their Collars, and their speeches to all the Savage nations of the Regions of the upper country, and who have Succeeded so well in their negotiations And in making them side with the English, that the Oataouas and Sauteux of Michillimaquinac Wished to Surprise that fort and Massacred several Frenchmen In various Places.

I Beg You to observe, Monseigner, that the cause, of all the ills and agitation of the upper country is due to the English who

3

have been left in peace at la Rivière Blanche; and all that evil was fomented there. In my memorial I took the liberty of suggesting to Your Grace Effective means for driving them away from there without occasioning any expenditure to the King either in troops or in money. I should have been pleased to have succeeded. At present the trouble Has become too great, the evil too Widespread, and The Savages have declared too openly In favor of the English to allow of its being undertaken.

I have obtained the knowledge of all this through Having Charge of the various Savage nations while I was Commandant at Niagara, where I applied myself Solely to Finding out their policy, their various interests, and in discovering their intrigues, and This had led me to foresee that they would be Corrupted and Won over by the English who trade at la Rivière Blanche, who have no other Object than to Make Themselves masters of all the upper country through the Sole medium of the Savages whose minds they have won by their address. I hope the evil will not become greater, but I should not Be Surprised if it did.

The only way to remedy it and to secure the fidelity of the Savages, the peaceful and Complete possession of all upper country, and the entire Trade with all the Savages that dwell there Is, therefore: to deprive them of all Communication with the English. To succeed in this, and to Establish a lasting peace in the whole of the upper country, let Your Grace make England Agree in the next treaty of peace with this Crown, that the English shall abandon and Give up to the King for ever the Complete possession of the fort of Chouégen; they Renounce having any relation with the Five yrocoisses nations, who shall remain subjects of His majesty; that they shall carry on no Trade either directly or indirectly throughout the territory Around lakes hontanriô, lake herrier, lake huron, Rivière Blanche and Belle Rivière; and that all the English trading at the said Rivière Blanche and Belle Rivière and in all there dependencies and other surrounding territories, shall Withdraw to their own country for ever Without ever being allowed to Return and carry on any Trade, or even Under any whatsoever.

By this means all the posts and upper countries will Be at peace and In Safety, the trade will become double what French have hitherto done, and will never again pass into hands of the

English.

With Regard to l'isle Royalle, the lands of la Cadie, and other places, I would not take the liberty of saying anything. You Know better than anybody, Monseigneur, what Should done for the Safety and advantage of the country. I most humbly Beg Your Grace to pardon me if I venture to make a few remarks Regarding the upper countries of This Colony; but I beg you At the same time to Observe that my zeal and my devotion to the King's Service have alone led me to take that liberty with The Sole desire to pay my respects to you, to deserve The honor of your Protection, and to assure you that I remain, with very profound Respect, Monseigneur, Your very humble And very obedient Servant,

De Raymond (Thwaites 1906:474-477).

The French saw not only the loss of trade along the Ohio River but also the expansionist/settlement tendency of the English, about which they continually warned the native people. The English would push north and west from Ohio to threaten Detroit and the Illinois country, eventually conquering the Great Lakes and the Mississippi River valley. As the Hudson's Bay Company already had them contained to the north, the French saw the real possibility of the French settlements in the St. Lawrence region being completely surrounded. History has proven this fear to be justified.

It is somewhat surprising that the French were able to act. The government of New France must have been suffering from some disruption due to a change in governors. Beauharnois had been replaced by La Jonquiere, who was an absentee administrator having been captured by the British. In his place, La Galissonière became temporary governor-general. Although he was to serve for a short period he had an impact on the situation. Beyond the immediate and pressing problems in the Ohio and Great Lakes, the new governor saw long term potential in the Illinois country.

M. DE LA GALISSONIÈRE TO COUNT DE MAUREPAS.

Quebec, 1st September, 1748.

My Lord.

In answer to one of your last despatches dated the 25th of April, and which reached me only by *Le Zephir*, I believe I have spoken to you somewhat at length of our Illinois establishments.

They possess this perhaps in common with all that relates to the Mississipi, that after having been praised greatly beyond their just value, scarcely a person can be found to-day who regards them as good for anything. I believe both extremes must be avoided, and here is what I think.

I regard the profits of the mines as very uncertain, and besides as so remote and dependent on as many other antecedent establishments, that no calculation can be made respecting them without, meanwhile, forever despairing of them.

I believe the fur trade carried on there one of the least advantageous in Canada, but I cannot speak with exactness.

The most I hope to draw from the country of the mines, is some bundles of buffalo skins.

I believe it extremely necessary that Louisiana be so settled as to derive flour and other life necessaries from points nearer than the Illinois.

In fine, I believe that it will be a long time before the King will realize any actual revenue, or individuals any considerable profit, from the Illinois; on the contrary, 'twill cost the King something to settle it.

But for all that, I am very far from concluding that the whole of that little Colony ought be left to perish. On the contrary, I consider that the King must make some sacrifice for its support.

P^{mo} So as not to lose what has been already expended there as a Colony.

2. Because it is one of the best situated barriers that can be opposed to the ambition of the English, to prevent them penetrating into our trading countries, and even into Mexico.

3. Because, were that country well settled, it would render us formidable to all the nations on the lower division of the River

Mississipi.

4. Because bread, meat and other provisions will attract thither the Indians, whose alliance and trade will be useful to us.

5. Had there been, for example, 400-500 men capable of bearing arms in the Illinois, this war, not only would our small posts of 8ahache (Wabash), & c., not have been disturbed, but the very nations who have frequently insulted us, would have been led even into the heart of the most flourishing English Colonies.

And here it is well to remark, that we must not flatter ourselves that our Continental Colonies; that is to say, this and Louisiana, can ever compete in wealth with the adjoining English Colonies, nor even carry on any very lucrative trade; for, except peltry, the amount of which is limited, and whose profits are and will be always diminishing, we shall scarcely ever have it in our power to furnish any but similar commodities to those of Europe; we shall not be able to supply them at the same price, though mostly of inferior quality, and though ours is an immense country, we have no outlet except by two rivers equally out of the way, whose navigation is inconvenient and perilous.

We are reduced then to make the most of the principal advantage of the country, which is its extreme productiveness and the facility of feeding a great many there without almost any foreign labor.

France derives from itself and its other Colonies, every sort of production; this one will not produce for a long time anything but men, but if wanted, 'twill produce in a sufficiently short time, so great a number of these; that, far from fearing English Colonies or Indian tribes, she will be in a position to dictate the law to them. And it is proper to remark that these Colonies are so precious to England, that if once Canada be sufficiently powerful in men to endanger them, this apprehension would rather have the affect of preventing the English making, as they so often do, a bad use of their maritime power.

As these views, though remote, must, it appears to me, engage our attention, I see no settlement more urgent than that of the Illinois. It is a country easy to cultivate and to clear, and greatly coveted by our neighbors.

Already there are a goodly number of families there, and those who will follow by degrees are sure of provisions.

But it is very difficult, not to say impossible, to increase the Illinois much from the Mississipi, which is itself in want of population, and will, by the beauty of its climate and the vicinity of the sea, always rather attract people from the Illinois than the Illinois draw any from Louisiana.

If to this we add the difficulties of ascending the Mississipi; the facilities hostile tribes have of arresting your upward progress, and the convenience Canadian Traders possess of going to Illinois by four or five different routes, which cannot be all blocked at the same time, it will be seen that it is Canada which is to furnish this population; and this, 1 think, is the manner it can be done.

P^{mo} To send from Canada to the Illinois one or two officers, and a detachment of fifty or sixty soldiers, to serve under M. de Bertet's orders.

2. To send down to Louisiana the two companies actually at the Illinois, that is to say the officers and young men of these companies, for all the married soldiers and those who would wish to become farmers there, must be discharged and left in Illinois.

3. To send thirty or forty salt smugglers, yearly, to the Illinois, by way of Canada, beginning as soon as possible.

4. To afford some facilities to ten or twelve Canadian farmers, every year, to go and settle and take up land there.

5. According as the troops here would fill up, to increase the garrison at the Illinois, as far as one hundred men or more.

6. To recommend the officer, in command there, to favor agriculture much more than trade.

7. To provide for the export of flour, which might be in too great abundance in the country, in consequence of the closing of the river.

I have expressly provided that the officers to be sent thither should be under M. de Bertet's orders, for I do not think it easy to find an officer as capable as he of managing and perfecting this settlement. I know him only by the reputation I have heard of him, and from the accounts I have had of him since I came here; and if there be anything valuable and true in what I have stated above, it is derived from his letters.

It is there I also find a remark essential to the subject. Should populous Illinois be capable of harassing the English colonies, these possess scarcely less facilities for seizing the Illinois, if left in their present languishing condition. Of all the countries in our occupation, this is the one which they can invade most easily with the smallest force; and could they once succeed in thus intruding themselves between our two Colonies, the loss of the Mississipi and the ruin of the internal trade of Canada would be assured, and the Spanish Colonies, and even Mexico, be in very great danger.

The result of all this is, that by connecting the Illinois with Canada, little will be gained in the item of the expense of the troops, the number of which, it seems to me, must rather be increased than diminished. In other respects, they are absolutely necessary there to restrain the Indians, and sometimes the settlers, and to increase in time the number of these latter.

For want of sufficient soldiers M. de Bertet has been, during the entire war, in continual danger, from which he has extricated himself, principally by his good conduct, and in some degree by the help of the ammunition and goods transmitted to him from this place.

It is to be also remarked that this post being situate at the extremity of our two Colonies, the Coureurs de bois and other bad subjects usually take refuge there, where they would possess opportunities of creating a great deal of disorder, should the commanding officer not have means at hand to repress them.

Much is not to be expected from farming this post, which I believe would be completing its ruin; some money, at most, can be derived from licenses, or those who will obtain them can be obliged to transport ammunition, and I know not if that even can be effected.

I agree with you, my Lord, in opinion that it is a matter of indifference whether an officer from Canada, or an officer from Louisiana, command at the Illinois, as far as its settlement, or the defence or even the existence of Louisiana is concerned.

He can always have orders to send down to New Orleans the largest quantity of flour possible, and to procure for that city, and whatever is connected with it, all the assistance in his power.

In order that there should be abundance in that post, and that its settlement be promoted, I see no objection to the Governor of Mississipi as well as the Governor of Canada, granting, or even selling, Trading Licenses for that place, provided the price be low, as that will not give rise to any discussion (n'y aiant aura point de discution).

This, my Lord, is nearly what I can answer on the subject of the Illinois.

I defer to a future time treating of all the posts of Canada, and, moreover, take the liberty of requesting you to consult M. Hocquart on that matter, though we may not be precisely of the same opinion.

I am, with most profound respect, My Lord,
Your most humble and Most obedient Servant,
La Galissonière (O'Callaghan X. 1858:134-136).

La Galissonière took action to protect all of France's interests west of the Appalachian Mountains. He dispatched Celoron de Blainville and Father Bonnecamps, to show the flag and gather intelligence about English activity. As a result of their expedition, and his Canadian experience, La Galissonière issued a paper which, apparently, had a profound affect on French policy. A portion of La Galissonière's paper is included at the end of this introduction.

While Celoron was in Ohio, La Jonquiere finally arrived in Canada. He confirmed the actions taken by his temporary replacement and mentions the need for permanent posts in the Ohio country.

M. DE LA JONQUIERE TO THE MINISTER OF THE MARINE
[Margry, Discouveries des Français, VI, 727-728]

Quebec, September 20, 1749

The moment I received the letter that you did me the honor to write on May 4, relating to the tribe of savages who were withdrawing to Sonioto, I wrote to M. de Vaudreuil, governor of Louisiana, to inform him that I would make every effort to reunite these savages with the rest of their tribe and that I would work jointly with him. I left my letter in France and very likely it has been sent out to him. I have transmitted your letter to the Marquis de La Galissonière; he has told me that M. de Celoron's

10

detachment apparently will bring about this reunion, at least for a time, but for something permanent we must establish one or more trading Posts on the Belle Rivière or in its vicinity, and especially toward its headwaters. These posts might have the inconvenience of making contraband trade easier; he judges, however, that this ought to be risked, because without it the English would undoubtedly locate there, and through this would be in a position to penetrate to all our trading posts and cut the communication with Louisiana. On the return of Sieur de Celoron, I hope to give a more accurate and extensive account (Stevens 1941:26-27).

The English were aware of French strategic plans and specific actions including the Celoron expedition. This paragraph from a report to London illustrates the concern of one colony, New York, to new French establishments in their area of influence. The letter that follows, from Pennsylvania's governor to his counterpart in New York, suggests that colonial cooperation, at least in the sharing of intelligence, was possible.

GOVERNOR CLINTON TO THE LORDS OF TRADE,

Fort George in New York
17th October 1749

The French at this time (as will appear by the papers I formerly sent and others which I now enclose) are forming schemes for intercepting the British Commerce with all the Indian Nations, which lay to the Westward of His Majesty's Colonies. What I think of the greatest consequence is what the French Engineer proposes to the Govr of Canada of building a Fort on the South Side of Ontario Lake to intercept the trade of Oswego, where the King has a garrison on that Lake for supporting the Trade of this Province. No Fort can be built any where on the South side of Ontario Lake, but on the Lands belonging to the Five Nations, who by the Treaty of Utrecht are declared subjects of Great Britain and who for a further security have in a solemn manner yielded and sold it to the King: As things now stand should the French attempt to erect any Forts, or make any settlements, on

11

the South side of that Lake, it may not be in my power to prevent it (O'Callaghan VI. 1855: 529).

Philad^a October 2^d 1749

Sir

While the Deputys of the Six Nations were lately in the City I made it my business to enquire their sentim^{ts} upon the march of such a Body of Frenchmen to Ohio, but they had no other knowledge of it than what they gained after their coming into this Province, neither upon my own acquainting them with it did it seem to give them any uneasiness.

A few Days ago the Messenger I sent into that Country returned and gave me the following account of His transactions. That upon his Arrival at an Indian town, called Logg's Town, on a branch of Ohio, he learnt that about 200 French and thirty Indians were just departed from thence after having summon'd a Council of the Indians & made them a speech the purpose whereof, as nearly as he could collect, together with their answer is inclosed. Whereupon the Messenger gathered the Chiefs of the Indians together & acquainted them that he was sent by me to apprize them of a piece of intelligence I had received from Your Excell^y & to put them on their guard in case the French might make any attempt upon them, & so repeated the substance of Your letter to me on that Subject. That when he had delivered his message the Indians expressed great thankfulness to their Brothers of New York & Pensylvania for their care in sending them an account of the French coming among them at a time when they did not expect them. That the Indians in Genl were much displeased at the proceedings of the French, & while he was among them held a Council in which it was resolved to fall upon them and cut them off, but that he advised them not to proceed in that manner, until they were more fully convinced than by words, that the French intended by force to gain the Subjection of the Twitchwees & Wayandotts (two nations that live further down the River & who for two or three years past have dealt largely with our Traders) That with a good deal of difficulty he

12

got them disswaded from falling on the French at that time, but they were still determined to differ with them, if the Twitchwees and Wayandotte who had fortified themselves in their towns would begin to quarell, to which purpose he sent Deputys to Council with them, who were not returned when he came away. That in gen[l] he found the Indians in Ohio heartily in the interest of the English, & fully bent to quarell with the French if ever they came again in the same hostile manner.

The French Officer who commanded the party understanding it was chiefly with this Province that those Nations of Indians trafficked put into the hands of some of our traders three Copys of the inclosed Papers to be delivered me, by which you will perceive they have it much at heart to regain that branch of Trade, which was in a manner lost to them during the war, by their Disappointm[t] of regular Supplys of Goods from France; And at present from the Affection those Nations have entertained of the English on acco[t] of their more friendly and reasonable manner of dealing with them. Upon the receipt of these papers I was apprehensive our traders might for the future be molested in their trade to that Country by Monsieur's carrying his threats into execution, & thought it incumbent on me to apprise them of this piece of Intelligence, that they might take their Measures accordingly, but I found them so satisfied of the Friendship of the Indians, & so secure of their protection against the French that they are determined to prosecute their Trade among them, which has of late been a very valuable one.

I have sent by a sloop belonging to this City the Guns Your Excell[y] was so kind to assist this Province with at a time when they stood much in need of them, and am again requested to return you the grateful acknowledgm[nt] of the Gentlemen Associates of so great a favour. I have the honour to be, S[r]

Your most obed[t] hble Servt

James Hamilton (O'Callaghan VI. 1855:530-531).

The findings of the Ohio expedition contained in Celoron's and Bonnecamps' reports are reflected in the document that follows. The Marquis de La Galissonière presents a compelling argument for the importance of the Ohio River to the interests of the French colonies in North America. (This is only a portion of the Memoir. See O'Callaghan X. 1858:220-232.)

MEMOIR OF THE FRENCH COLONIES IN NORTH AMERICA BY THE MARQUIS DE LA GALISSONIÈRE.

December, 1750

What has been observed already in the course of this Memoir, when treating of the utility of Canada in regard to the preservation of Mexico, shows the absolute necessity of the free and certain communication from Canada to the Mississippi. This chain, once broken, would leave an opening of which the English would doubtless take advantage to get nearer the silver mines (la source de l'argent). Many of their writings are full of this project, which will never amount to anything but a chimera, if France retain her Canadian possessions.

That of the River Oyo, otherwise called the Beautiful River, is the most interesting in this relation. It rises near the country at present partly occupied by the Iroquois, runs southwardly, falls into the Ouabache, and with that river into the Mississippi.

This last has been discovered by Sieur De La Salle, who took possession of it in the King's name; and it would perhaps today be full of French settlements, had not the Governors of Canada been deterred from establishing permanent posts there by the apprehension that a contraband trade between the French traders and the English would be the consequence.

Neither have the English any posts there, nor did they come to that quarter to trade, except clandestinely, until the last war, when the revolt of some neighboring nations against the French, encouraged them to come more boldly.

They have been summoned since the peace, to retire, and if they do not do so, there is no doubt but the Governor of Canada will constrain them thereto by force, otherwise the case would be the same as at Chouaguen, and this misfortune would be still more disastrous, for a post on the Beautiful River would possess more opportunities to do damage than Chouaguen alone.

1st. They would have much greater opportunities there than

14

at Chouaguen to seduce the Indian nations.

2nd. They would possess more facilities to interrupt the communication between Canada and Louisiana, for the Beautiful River affords almost the only route for the conveyance from Canada to the River Mississippi, of detachments capable of securing that still feeble Colony against the incursions of the neighboring Indians of Carolina, whom the English are unceasingly exciting against the French.

3rd. If the English ever become strong enough in America to dare attempt the conquest of Mexico, it will be by this Beautiful River, which they must necessarily descend.

4th. By it alone will they also be able to attack, with any considerable force, and any hope of success, the Illinois posts and all those which will be established along the River St. Louis, or Mississippi.

5th. It is, moreover, by that route that they can attack the post of the Miamis, which, again, cuts off one of our best communications with the River Mississippi, and involves the loss of Detroit, an important post whereof mention will be made hereafter.

The establishment of some posts on the Beautiful River is considered, then, one of the most urgent expenses; but 'tis believed, at the same time, that these posts will not acquire any solidity except so far as the strength of Niagara and Detroit will be augmented.

The importance of the Ohio River was clear to both French and English authorities. What remained was the commitment to act decisively. The documents below leave little doubt as to the wishes of the King. They also reflect the persuasiveness of the arguments put forth by La Galissonière and La Jonquière.

MINISTERIAL MINUTE ON THE ATTEMPTS OF THE ENGLISH TO SETTLE ON THE OHIO.

CANADA.

The English always occupied with plans to extend their possessions, and to confine those of his Majesty, in North America, have undertaken since the last war to carry their trade towards the Beautiful river, which is situated in the interior, between Canada and Louisiana, and forms the principal communication between these two Colonies; to corrupt the Indian Nations of that quarter, and even to establish posts there.

The Marquis de la Jonquière having been informed of those attempts, adopted measures last year to prevent their success. He organized divers detachments of Frenchmen and Indians, which, according to his arrangements, were to form a junction this spring to proceed at once to the Beautiful river, drive the English from it, and bring back the Indians who might have allowed themselves to be debauched by the intrigues of that Nation.

News of the result was expected at the end of this year, but private letters have arrived from Canada stating that the Marquis de la Jonquière has abandoned that project, and insinuating that private interest has led some one, in whom he had placed his confidence, to dissuade him from it, by making him apprehend creating thereby a general Indian war.

This motive would be good, if it were valid. It is proper always to avoid, as much as possible, war with the Indians; but, it appears, that an this occasion, it was not difficult to guarantee himself against it.

The question is not to operate against the Indians, but to prevent the interloping trade the English are driving in a country belonging to us, and which, previous to the last war, they would be careful not to dispute us; this is proposed to be effected by checking at the same time the views they entertain of establishing posts there. It is easy, therefore, to render the Indians indifferent in this regard; nay, even to induce them to understand that for the sake of their own tranquillity and of the freedom of their trade, in which we have never clogged them, they must wish that we should stop the progress of the English schemes.

'T'would therefore be unfortunate if the Marquis de la Jonquière has abandoned the project he had formed for that purpose; and although the private advices announcing that change on his part may be unfounded, it appears, nevertheless, proper not to keep him in ignorance of them; to inform him, at the same time, that his Majesty continues to expect the execution of this project; that there is, in fact; no other course to adopt than to drive from the Beautiful river any European foreigners who will happen to be there, so as to make them lose all taste for returning thither, observing, notwithstanding, the caution practicable in these sorts of matters.

As for the rest, there is no reason to apprehend any justifiable complaints on the part of the Court of England. The French were the discoverers of the beautiful river, which has always served as a communication, as already observed, between Canada and Louisiana. We always carried on trade there without any interruption, and have sent considerable detachments thither on various occasions.

23^d September, 1751(O'Callaghan X. 1858:239-240).

MINISTERIAL MINUTE ON THE ENGLISH ENCROACHMENTS ON THE OHIO.

Canada, 1752.

The Marquis de la Jonquière reported last year that the Indian Nations of the Upper countries were threatening a sort of general conspiricy against the French, and that the English who succeeded in debauching them by presents and intrigues, were pledged to sustain them by arms.

He stated, at the same time, that the reports made to him by some faithful Nations, caused him to conclude that effectual measures must be indispensably adopted, both to bring the nations that had joined the conspiracy, back to their attachment to France, or to oblige them to return to their duty, and to destroy, by force of arms, the posts the English might have undertaken to erect on our territory toward the River Oio, whence they set all these movements on foot; and this Governor transmitted at the same time, a plan of operations which he was to execute, and which consisted principally in dispatching at the beginning of autumn last year, several detachments for various posts, whence they were to make a junction at the opening of the spring, at a Rendezvous indicated to them, to act according to circumstances.

We learned by letters received from the Marquis de la Jonquière, and dated last September, that his plan was badly executed and the officers entrusted with its execution had undertaken nothing against the rebellious Indians, nor against the English posts, and that the movements of those Indians are every day becoming more dangerous.

The Marquis de la Jonquière states, however, that he does not despair of reëstablishing tranquillity in the Upper Country; he has adopted new measures for that purpose, and explains the details thereof in the annexed letter.

Meanwhile, he has caused the arrest of 4 Englishmen who were trading on the lands of the Colony, and were endeavoring to debauch our Indians. It appears from the interrogatories they were subjected to at Quebec, that they were authorized by the English Governors, though they had not, however, produced their passports. The Marquis de la Jonquière has sent three of them to France, the 4th being unable, from sickness, to embark. Those three have been imprisoned at Rochelle, and 'tis proper that they be left there. It is not expected that the Court of England will reclaim them; at least they have not claimed that class of prisoners who have been taken in Louisiana, some years before the last war, and sent to France. But at all events, should any complaint be made on the subject, it will be easy to give an answer to it. As for the rest, the seizure of these trading posts is the least expensive, least inconvenient, and perhaps the most effectual way to put a stop, in the Indian country, to the movements the English are endeavoring to excite there (O'Callaghan X. 1858:240-241).

The focus for the French, confirmed by King, was eliminating English influence among the nations on the Ohio River and effectively blocking their reentry. The English, already established, needed to maintain the route from the east to the tribes. The French acted first by targeting the English trading center at Pickawillany, the hub of activity in the Ohio River Valley. An expedition to destroy Pickawillany in 1751, failed. It was attempted again, the next year. Charles Mouet de Langlade led a force of Indians, mostly Ottawas (his mother's people), in an attack that destroyed the village. This action greatly disrupted English trade and influence, but did not eliminate it.

The next goal was to block English reentry and expansion. Both powers looked toward the forks of the Ohio, the junction of the Allegheny River and the Monongahela River. This was the entry point for traders from Pennsylvania, Virginia, and Maryland. The establishment of a fortified post at this site would control access to the west. Colonial traders, John Fraser and Christoper Gist, had already constructed buildings in this region. Yet, the first power to establish a military presence at this site would determine control of the territory.

In 1753, French forces landed in the north at Presque Isle (Erie, Pennsylvania). They established a fort, Presque Isle, on Lake Erie and another, Fort LeBoeuf (Waterford, Pennsylvania), at the south end of a portage to the headwaters of French Creek. This stream flowed into the Allegheny River at Venango (Franklin, Pennsylvania), where Celoron had buried a lead plate and found cabins belonging to John Fraser. Before winter, the French established a small garrison using Fraser cabins and fortified it (Fort Machault) the next year. The goal of building a fort at the Forks of the Ohio would have to wait until 1754.

The British knew of the French activity and decided to enter the game. George Washington was dispatched by Governor Dinwiddie of Virginia to tell the French to leave English land. It is doubtful that Dinwiddie believed his warning would have any effect. It was, however, a gentlemanly gesture, and it provided an excellent excuse to gather intelligence. Washington's report of his Pennsylvania adventure accelerated an effort be first on the Ohio. Weather conditions gave the English an advantage. Following the Spring weather north, they arrived at the forks of the Ohio before the French.

The effort was insufficient. In April 1754, as English colonial troops began building a fort on the Ohio, they looked up to see a large French

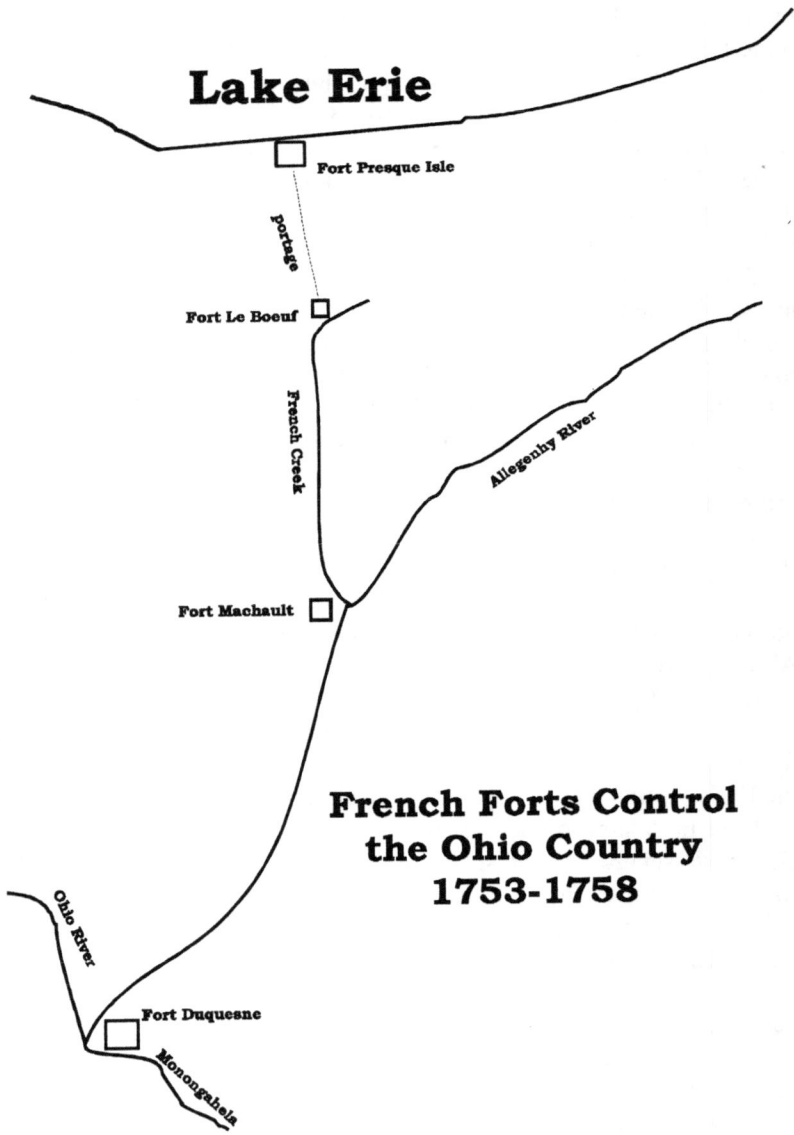

Lake Erie

Fort Presque Isle

portage

Fort Le Boeuf

French Creek

Allegenhy River

Fort Machault

French Forts Control the Ohio Country 1753-1758

Ohio River

Fort Duquesne

Monongahela

force begin to mount cannon on carriages in range of their partially finished wooden stockade. The French sent a message stating their opinion concerning ownership of this region. Out manned and out gunned, the English left. The French continued a little further downstream and began constructing Fort Duquesne.

The French establishment led to further actions, accidents, and incidents. The highlights of these are the attack on the Jumonville party and the surrender of Fort Necessity in 1754. The following year, the Battle of the Monongahela (Braddock's defeat) was the result of another attempt to achieve dominion over the Ohio. In 1758, Forbes' expedition finally took the forks of the Ohio from the French. When Fort Niagara was captured by the English in 1759, their dominion over the Ohio was greatly reinforced. The surrender of Canada in 1760, settled the issue. These highlights, of course, are part of the final French and Indian War.

Where does the Celoron Expedition fit into the pageant of history? It was certainly part of the action leading to the final French and Indian War. The journals that follow provide a picture of what actually happened during those months of 1749. They also provide an insight into the French viewpoint of their relations with the English and the native people. This allows a deeper understanding of the conditions that led to war in the Ohio country, that led to a general North American conflict, that led to a European war, spreading to other colonies around the globe.

CELORON'S JOURNAL

Journal of the expedition which I, Celoron,[1] Knight of the Royal and Military Order of St. Louis,[2] Captain, commanding a detachment sent down the Beautiful River[3] by the orders of M., the Marquis de La Galissonière,[4] Governor-General of all New France, and of the Country of Louisiana.

I set out from La Chine[5] on the 15th of June with a detachment composed of one Captain, eight subaltern officers, six Cadets[6], one Chaplain,[7] twenty soldiers, one hundred and eighty Canadians, and about thirty Indians, there being as many Iroquois[8] as Abenakis.[9] I passed the night at Point Claire.[10] The 16th, I set out at ten in the morning and passed the night at Soulange, with my whole detachment; several canoes were destroyed in the rapids. The 17th, I set out from Soulange, I ascended the Cedars,[11] the rapids of the lake, to where M. Joncaire[12] made shipwreck, his canoe being broken, one man drowned, and the greater part of the goods lost. The 18th, I stopped at the entrance of Lake St. Francis in order to get the few goods dried, which had been gathered up at the foot of the rapids. The 19th, I passed Lake St. Francis, and ascended the rapids, called the Thousand Rocks, making the passage without accident. The 20th, I ascended the long bottom. The 21st, I passed several rapids, I'll not give the number of them, they are known to every one. The 22d, 23d and 24th, I continued my route without anything remarkable having happened, save that several canoes were smashed through the ill-will of those who were guiding them; I got them repaired, and continued my route. I passed the 25th at a new French establishment which M. the abbe Piquet[13] founded, where I found about sixty acres of cleared land. His stone fort, eight feet high, was not as yet much advanced. The abbe Piquet lodged in a bark cabin in the Indian fashion, and had lumber and other materials prepared for his lodging; he had two Montagnes[14] Indians who besought me to take them along with me. To please him I accepted them. This was all that made up his mission. The 26th, I set out from M. Piquet's and passed the night at the Narrows. The 27th, I set out early in the morning to go to Fort Frontenac[15] where I arrived at five in the evening. The 28th and 29th, I stopped at Fort Frontenac to repair my canoes, which had been very much damaged in the rapids, and to give my men a rest. The 30th, I set out from Fort Frontenac to go to Niagara. At Quinte[16] I fell in with Monsieur de la Naudiere[17] who was returning from the Miamis.[18] He told me that the nations of Detroit,[19] apprised of my expedition, were ready on the first invitation to come and join me. I did not count much on the disposition of these Indians; however, as I had learned on my route that there would be more people on the Beautiful River than had been reported to M. de La Galissonière, I profited, at all risks, by the advice of M. de la Naudiere, and forced my voyage to rejoin M. de Sabrevois[20] who was going as Commander to Detroit: the 6th of July I arrived at Niagara[21] where I found him. We conversed together, and I wrote to M. the chevalier Longueuil[22] what I had learned from M. de la Naudiere, and I begged him, that if the nations of Detroit had the intention of coming to join me, not to be slow in telling them to set out; that I appointed the place of meeting at St. Yotoc from the 9th to the 12th of August; that if they had change their intention I would feel obliged to him to send me scouts to inform me of their plans, so as to know what I ought to do. The 7th of July, I had M. de Contrecoeur,[23] Captain and second in command of the detachment, to set out with Messrs. the subaltern officers and all my canoes, to go make the portage. I stayed at the fort awaiting my Indians, who had taken a different route from mine in Lake Ontario. They having rejoined me, I went to the portage which M. de Contrecoeur had made. The 14th of the same month I entered Lake Erie, where a strong gale made me encamp at some leagues above the little rapids; there I had some piquets[24] formed to keep sentry, which consisted of forty men commanded by an officer. The 15th, I set out at early morning in the hope of having a fine day and of arriving at the Portage of Chatakuin,[25] which I was not able to do; a strong gale having risen, just as on the previous day, I was obliged to go ashore. The lake is extremely shallow, there is no protection, and if you did not sail before the wind you would run the risk of perishing when landing. Large rocks are found to a distance of more than three-fourths of a mile from the shore, upon which you are in danger of perishing. I fell upon one, and without prompt assistance I should have been drowned with all on board.

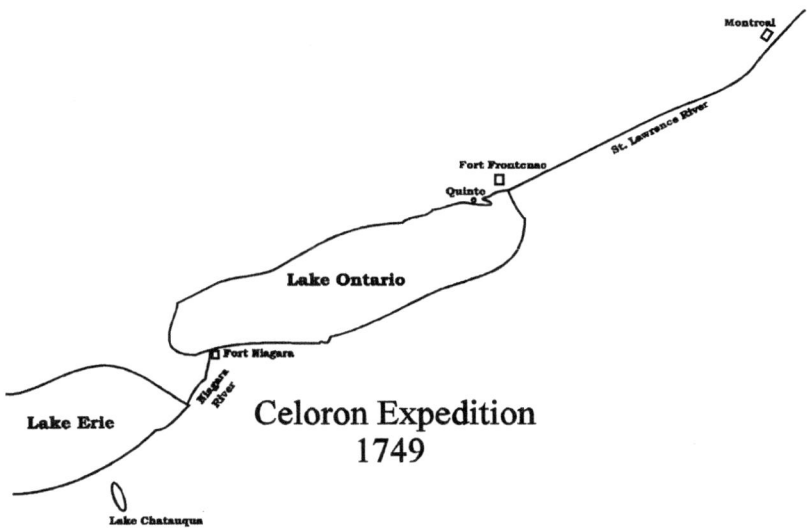

Montreal

St. Lawrence River

Fort Frontenac

Quinto

Lake Ontario

Fort Niagara

Niagara River

Lake Erie

**Celoron Expedition
1749**

Lake Chatauqua

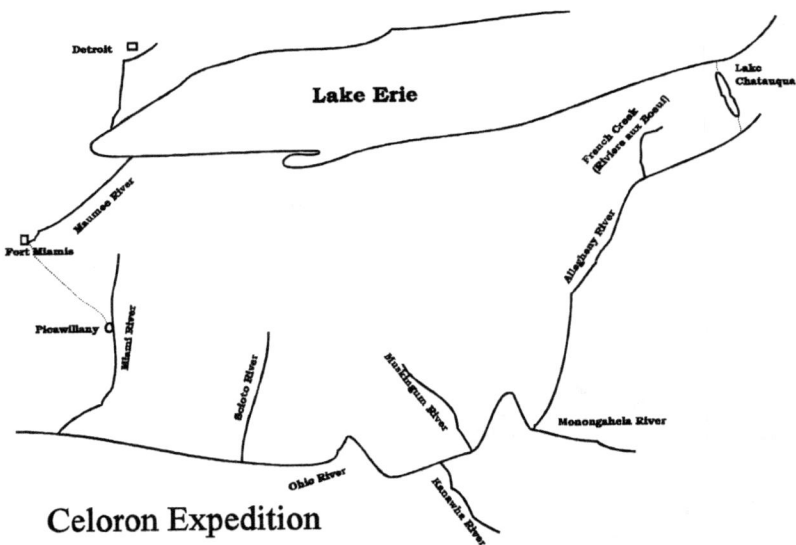

Detroit

Lake Erie

Lake
Chatauqua

French Creek
(Rivière aux Boeuf)

Maumee River

Allegheny River

Fort Miamis

Picawillany

Miami River

Scioto River

Muskingum River

Monongahela River

Ohio River

Kanawha River

Celoron Expedition
1749

26

I landed to repair my canoe which had been broken in several places. The 16th, at noon, I arrived at the portage of Chatakuin. As soon as all my canoes were loaded, I despatched M. de Villiers[26] and M. le Borgne[27] with fifty men to go clear a road. The rest of the day I made observations on the situation of the place, in case that I might afterwards wish to establish a post there; I found nothing there of advantage either for the navigation of the lake, or for the situation of the post; the lake is so shallow on the side of the south, that ships could not approach the portage but at more than a league's distance. There is no island or harbor where they could be moored and put under protection; they must needs remain at anchor and have boats for unloading them; the gales of wind are so frequent there that I think they would be in danger. Besides, there is no Indian village established in this place; they are at a great distance, the nearest are those of Ganaouagon[28] and of the Cut Straw[29]. In the evening Messrs. de Villiers and Le Borgne[30] came to pass the night in the camp, having cleared about three-quarters of a league of the road. Sentinels were placed, and this order continued during the whole campaign, as much for the safety of the detachment as for forming the Canadians to discipline, of which they stood in need. The 17th, at break of day, we commenced our portage which was vigorously prosecuted, since all the canoes, provisions, munitions of war and merchandise destined as presents for the nations of the Beautiful River, were carried the three-quarters of a league[31] which had been cleared the day previous. This road is very difficult by reason of numerous hills and mountains which are met with thereon; our men were also very tired. The 18th, I continued my portage, but the bad weather hindered me from pushing on as far as the preceding day. I consoled myself for this delay; being only prevented by the rain, it was all that I wished, so as to have water in the river for passing with the loads which I had in my canoes. The 19th, the rain having abated I resumed the march, and that day made half a league. The 20th and 21st, we continued our route with great haste. The 22d, we finished the portage which may he counted as four leagues, and we arrived at the head of the Lake Chataquin; at this place I had my canoes repaired, and allowed my men to repose. At noon on the 22d, I set out and encamped at the outlet of the lake, which may have been nine leagues. In the evening our Indians, who had been fishing in the lake, told me that they had seen people who concealed themselves in the woods as soon as they had been perceived. The 24th, I departed from the lake at an early enough hour in the morning, and we entered the river of Chatakuin. The water being rather low I had the greater part of the baggage transported by hand. The portage was pointed out to me by the S. de la Saussaye.[32] It was almost three-quarters of a league. This transport rendered easy the passage of our canoes which could not have passed with the loads. We made almost half a league this day by water. The 25th, before setting out on the march, at the representations of the Indians of my detachment, I called a council composed of Messrs. the officers and the nations I had with me to deliberate together upon the measures we ought to take on the occasion of the vestiges we had found the day before of several cabins abandoned with so much precipitation that the Indians had left behind a part of their utensils, their canoes, and even their provisions, to seek the woods. This action gave us proof of the terror of these Indians, and that they withdrew only through fear, and that they would consequently bear the alarm into all the villages, would put them also to flight, or make them adopt the plan of assembling to form considerable bodies, and lay an ambush for us. The country was extremely advantageous for them, and for us of very difficult access on account of the small amount of water there was in the river. I communicated the intentions of M. the Marquis de La Galissonière to the officers, who saw that it was of great importance for the execution of the orders with which I was charged, to reassure the nations of these countries; and the unanimous sentiment was, to send them word to remain quiet in their cabins and to assure them that I came only to treat with them of good things and to explain to them the sentiments of their Father, Onontio.[33] I had their opinions drawn out in writing, which they all signed. The following is a copy of them:

Council held by M. de Celoron with Messrs. the officers of his detachment and the chiefs, the 25th of July, 1749.

Having discovered on the 24th of July at the lower part of the Lake Chatakuin vestiges by which it appeared to us that the Indians who were on the hunt in this place had been frightened at the number of canoes and people that composed our detachment, having abandoned their canoes, provisions, and other utensils, and that they had gone to carry the alarm to the village of the Cut Straw; and as it is important in consequence of the orders of M. the Marquis de La Galissonière to speak to these nations to make known to them his intentions, and not wishing to do anything without the advice of Messrs. the officers and the chiefs whom we have with us, we have assemble them to communicate to them the orders with which we are charged, so as to adopt together the most suitable measures to dissipate the terror which our march has spread. The opinions of all having been received, the unanimous sentiment was, that to reassure these nations and have an opportunity to speak to them, a canoe should be, told off to go to the village of the Cut Straw, in which should embark M. de Joncaire, Lieutenant,[34] with two Abenakis and three Iroquois to carry them three belts of wampum, and induce them to take courage, that their father came only to treat with them of good things.

Made at our Camp at the entrance of the River of Chatakuin, this 25th of July, 1749 All the officers signed.

As soon as the council was ended, I made M. de Joncaire set out. This done, I set out and made about a league with much difficulty. In many places I was obliged to assign forty men to each canoe to have them pass over. The 26th, 27th and 28th, I continued my voyage, not without many obstacles; and despite all the precautions I took to manage my canoes, they often sustained great injury on account of the dearth of water. The 29th, at noon, I entered the Beautiful River. I had a leaden plate buried on which was engraved the taking possession which I made, in the name of the King, of this river and of all those which fall into it. I had also attached to a tree the arms of the King, struck on a plate of sheet iron, and of all this I drew up an official statement, which Messrs. the officers and I have signed.

Copy of written record of the position of the leaden plate and of the arms of the King, deposited at the entrance of the Beautiful River, together with the inscription:

In the year one thousand seven hundred and forty-nine, we Celoron, Knight of the Royal Military Order of St. Louis, Captain commanding a detachment sent by the orders of M. the Marquis de La Galissonière, Governor-General of New France, on the Beautiful River, otherwise called the Oyo, accompanied by the principal officers of our detachment, buried at the foot of a red oak, on the southern bank of the river Oyo and of Kanaougon, and at 42 degrees 5' 23" a leaden plate, with this inscription thereon engraven:

INSCRIPTION

In the year 1749, in the reign of Louis the XV, King of France, we, Celoron, commander of ·the detachment sent by M. de la Galissonière, Governor-General of New France, to reestablish peace in some villages of these Cantons, have buried this plate at the confluence of the Ohio and the Kanaaiagon, the 29th of July, for a monument of the renewal of possession which we have taken of the said river Ohio, and of all those which fall into it, and of all the territories on both sides as far as the source of the said rivers, as the preceding Kings of France have possessed or should possess them, and as they are maintained therein by arms and by treaties, and especially by those of Riswick, Utrecht and of Aix la Chapelle; have moreover affixed to a tree the arms of the King. In testimony whereof, we have drawn up and signed the present written record. Made at the entrance of the Beautiful River, the 29th Of July, 1749. All the officers signed.

This ceremony over, as I was not far distant from the village of Kanaouagon, and as the Indians were notified by M. de Joncaire of my arrival, they were on the watch to discover me. As soon as they had descried my canoes, they sent me a deputation to invite me to come to their villages and to receive there the compliments of their Chiefs. I treated well those sent. I made them drink a draught of the milk[35] of their Father Onontio, and gave them tobacco. They returned to their villages, and I followed a short time after. I passed before the village; they saluted me with several discharges of musketry; I returned the salutes, and encamped on the other side of the river. M. de Joncaire brought the Chiefs to my tent; I received their felicitations, and as this village consists of twelve or thirteen cabins, I invited them to come to the Cut Straw to hear what I had to say to them on the part of their father Onontio. The women brought me presents of Indian corn and squashes, for which I gave them little presents. M. de Joncaire assured me that it was well that he had gone in advance to dispel the terror which had seized the Indians; that several had withdrawn into the woods, and that the others had prepared to follow. I made M. de Joncaire set out for the Cut Straw. The

30

30th, I betook myself to Cut Straw whither I had sent M. de Joncaire the previous day. The Indians of this place had formed the design of fleeing into the woods on the report which those had given them, who had descried us in the Lake Chatakuin, who had told them that we were a considerable force, and that, undoubtedly, it was our intention to destroy them. M. de Joncaire found much difficulty in removing this impression, although they were Iroquois of the Five Nations which composed these two villages; although he is in fact adopted by the nation, and they have great confidence in him. As soon as I arrived the Chiefs assembled and came to my tent.

The following is their opening speech: Speech of the Sonontouans[36] established at the village of Cut Straw, otherwise called Kachinodiagon, and of Kanaouagon, to M. de Celoron, accompanied by two belts of wampum, the 30th day of July, 1749·

"My Father, we come to give testimony of the joy which we feel at seeing you arrived at our villages in good health. It is a long time since we have had the pleasure of seeing our Father in these territories, and the expedition of which we have been apprised for a month has caused much uneasiness and fear not only in our villages, but in all those of the Beautiful River. Thou hast perceived it, my Father, and to reassure thy children, frightened and without courage, thou hast done well to send us our son Joncaire to tell us to be calm and to await in our villages thy arrival, to hear the word of our father Onontio, which thou bringest us. The belts of wampum have entirely calmed our mind of all the fears which had seized on us; our bundles were prepared for fleeing, and we were like drunken people. All has passed away, and we have remained as thou wished it to hear what thou hast to tell us. We are delighted that father Onontio has made choice of thee to make his intentions known to us. It is not to-day that we know thee; thou didst govern us at Niagara, and thou knowest that we never did aught but thy will."

Answer of M. de Celoron to the above speech, accompanied by three belts of wampum, the 30th of July, 1749:

"I am delighted, my children, that the arrival of M. de Joncaire in your villages has calmed your minds, and has dispelled the fears which my expedition into this country has caused you. No doubt but it was occasioned by the sinister conduct of people who always occupy themselves in evil designs. What surprises me is, that those who have a right spirit, and who have always listened to the words of their father Onontio, have caused this fear. By these three belts of wampum I open your ears so that you may hear well what I have to say to you on the part of your father Onontio, and that I may also open your eyes to make you see clearly the advantages which your father wishes to procure you, if like sensible people you wish to avail yourselves of them. It is his word which I bring you here, and which I am going to bring to all the villages of the Beautiful River."

Words of M. the Marquis de La Galissonière to the first village of the Iroquois Sonontuerna, established at the entrance of the Beautiful River, delivered by M. de Celoron:

"My children, since I began to wage war with the English I have learned that this nation has seduced you, and that not content with corrupting your heart, they have profited of the time of my absence from this country to invade the territories which do not belong to them, and which are mine; a circumstance which has determined me to send M. de Celoron to you, to make known my intentions, which are, that I will not suffer the English in my territories; and I invite you, if you are my real children to receive them no more into your villages. I cut off, then, by this belt, the commerce which they have lately established in this part of the country, and I announce to you that I will not suffer them there any more. If you are attached to me, you will make them withdraw, and will send them home; by this means you will always be in peace in your villages. I will grant you for this all the aid you have a right to expect from a good father. Come to see me next spring; you will have reason to be pleased with the reception I will give you; I will abundantly furnish you with traders, if you desire it; I will even add officers to them, if that gives you pleasure, to lead you and to give you courage, so that you engage only in lawful business. The English have acted all the more wrongly in coming into these territories, as the Five Nations[37] have forbidden them to remain beyond the mountains. Pay serious attention, my children, to the message which I send you. Listen to it well; follow it, it is the means of always seeing over your villages a beautiful and serene sky. I expect suitable from you an answer worthy of my true children. You will see marks which I have fixed along the Beautiful River, which will prove to the English that this land belongs to me, and that they cannot come into it without exposing themselves to be expelled from it. This time I desire to treat them with kindness and if they are wise they will profit by my advice."

Two belts of wampum.

"I am surprised, my children, to see raised in your village a cabin destined to receive English traders. If you look upon yourselves as my children you will not continue this work; far from it, you will destroy it, and will no longer receive the English at your homes."

Answer of the Iroquois of the villages of Ganaouskon and of Chinodiagon, the 31st of July, 1749; with two belts of wampum:

"My father, we thank you for having opened our ears and our eyes to understand your speech, and see clearly that you speak to us as a good father.

A belt.

"My father, we are very glad to speak to-day of business with you. Do not be surprised at our answers; we are people who have no knowledge of business, but who speak to you from the bottom of their heart. My father, you have appeared to us surprised at this that the English came for commerce upon our lands. It is true our old men forbade their entrance. You engage us to go up to Montreal next year so as to speak of business with Onontio, and we appreciate these favors. We assure you that we are going to prepare for this during the winter, and that we will go next spring.

"My father, you have told us that you perceive that the English came to invade our lands, and that you have come to summon them to withdraw; that to the end you closed the way against them. We thank you for your undertaking, and we promise you no more to suffer them here. We are not a party capable of deciding entirely on the general sentiment of the Five Nations who inhabit this river. We await the decisions of the Chiefs of our villages, as also the villages lower down. For us, my father, we assure you that we will not receive the English into our two villages.

Two belts of wampum:

"My father, you have told us that some little birds had given you word that a house was being built for the English, and that if we suffered them to do so, they would shortly raise here a considerable establishment for driving us away, because they would render themselves masters of our lands. You have invited us to discontinue this work. This is what we promise you, and this house which is almost finished, will serve only for a recreation place for the youth. We promise you also not to touch the arms of the King which you have planted on this river, and which will prove to the English that they have no right in this part of the country.

Two belts of wampum to the Indians of the detachment.

"My brothers, we are delighted to see you accompany our father on his voyage; you have told us that you have no other sentiments than those of Onontio. We invite you to follow the counsels which he desires to give you, and we have taken the resolution to do only his will. We thank you for what you have told us, and we will pay attention to it."

The council over, I made presents to the Indians, which gave them great pleasure; and in return they assured me anew that they would never receive the English in their homes, and that they would go down next spring to see their father Onontio.

The 31st of July I sojourned at this village, having been delayed by an abundant fall of rain, which gave us a great deal of pleasure; the river rose three feet during the night. The 1st of August I set out from the Cut Straw. After having gone about ten leagues, I found a village of Loups[38] and Renards[39] of about ten cabins. I landed, and found only one man, who told me that the rest had fled. I told the Indian that his people were wrong to let themselves be frightened, that I did not come to do them harm; far from it, but I came to treat with them of good things, and to encourage the children of the Governor, who were in need of it. I added that I did not doubt but that as soon as their fear was over, they would return home; that I invited them to come to the village lower down, which was not further than four or five leagues, and that I would speak to them. This same day I passed by a little village of six cabins, the inhabitants of which I told, as I had the others, to come to the most considerable village, where I would speak to them on the part of their father Onontio. They arrived there a short time after me. The 2d, I spoke to the Indians in the name of M. the Governor. following are the speech and their answer:

A belt.

"My children, the Loups, the reason which determined your father Onontio to send me into this part of the country, was the information he had received that the English proposed to form posts considerable enough to invade one day these lands and to increase therein in such a way, if they were let do so, that they would render themselves masters of them, and you would be the victims. As you have in the past heard with attention the word which I bring you on his part, the experience you have had, my children, of the evil intentions of the English in your regard ought always to be remembered. Remember that you formerly possessed at Philadelphia, beautiful lands, upon which you found in abundance wherewith to sustain your families. They drew near you under pretext of ministering to your wants, and little by little, without you perceiving it, they established forts and afterwards towns, and when they grew powerful enough, they drove you away and forced you to come and establish yourselves on these lands, to find subsistence for your wives and your children. What they did at Philadelphia they purposed doing to-day upon the Beautiful River by the posts which they wish to establish there. It is the knowledge which I have of this, seeing farther than you, which has determined me to send you M. de Celoron to make you open your eyes to the evils which threaten you, and to make you see that it is personal interest alone that influences the English. I send to summon them for this time to withdraw, not wishing that they occupy the lands which belong to me; if they are prudent they will not expose themselves to be forced to it. The English have much less right to come since the Kings of France and England have agreed in all the treaties of peace, and particularly in the last which terminated the war, that the English should never put their foot on these lands. You know also, my children, that the Five Nations have absolutely forbidden them, not only to establish posts upon the Beautiful River, but even to come there to trade; that they remain on the other side of the mountains on the land which they have usurped from you. To this I am not opposed, but on my lands I shall not suffer them. For you, my children, you will lose nothing thereby; far from it, I will give you all the aid you have a right to expect from a good father. Depute next spring some persons of your nation with your old men to come and see me, and you will see by the reception I will give you, how much I love you, and that I seek only to do you good and to free you from the yoke of the English which they still wish to impose on you. I will give you traders who will supply all your wants and put you in such a state as not to regret those whom I remove from your lands. These lands which you possess you will be always masters of."

Answer of the Loups the 2d of August:

A belt.

"My father, we pray you have pity on us, we are young men who cannot answer you as old men would. What you have said has opened our eyes and given us courage. We see that you labor only for our good, and we promise you to entertain no other sentiments than those of our uncles, the Five Nations, with whom you seem pleased. Consider, my father, the situation in which we are placed. If you compel the English to retire, who minister to our wants, and in particular the blacksmith who mends our guns and our hatchets, we shall be forced to remain without succor and be exposed to the danger of dying of hunger and misery on the Beautiful River. Have pity on us, my father, you cannot at present minister to our wants, let us have, during this winter, or at least till we go hunting, the blacksmith and some one who can aid us. We promise you that by spring the English shall retire."

I told them, without making them any promise, that I would make an arrangement which would best suit their interests and the intentions of their father Onontio. I confess that their reply embarrassed me very much. I made them a little present, and induced them to keep the promise which they had given me. The 3d I set out on the route. On the way I found a village of ten abandoned cabins, the Indians, having been apprised of my arrival, had gained the woods. I continued my route as far as the village at the River aux Boeufs,[40] which is only of nine or ten cabins. As soon as

36

they perceived me they fired a salute. I had their salute returned, and landed. As I had been informed that there was at this place a blacksmith and an English merchant, I wished to speak to them; but the English, as well as the Indians, had gained the woods. There remained only five or six Iroquois, who presented themselves with their arms in their hands. I rebuked them for their manner of showing themselves, and made them lower their arms. They made many excuses, and told me they would not have come with their guns, except that they had them to salute me. I spoke to them in almost the same terms as I had done to the Loups, and immediately embarked. That evening I had a leaden plate buried, and had the arms of the king attached to a tree; and drew up the following official statement of the transaction:

OFFICIAL STATEMENT.

In the year 1749, we, Celoron. Knight of the Royal and Military order of St. Louis, Captain commanding the detachment sent by the orders of M, the Marquis de la Galissonière, Governor-General of New France, on the Beautiful River, otherwise called the Ohio, accompanied by the principal officers of our detachment, have buried upon the southern bank of the Ohio, at four leagues distance below the River aux Boeufs, directly opposite a naked mountain, and near an immense stone upon which certain figures are rudely enough carved, a leaden plate, and have attached in the same place to a tree the arms of the king. In testimony whereof we have signed the present official statement. Made at our camp the 3d of August, 1749. All the officers signed.

The inscription is the same as the preceding one, which I placed at the entrance of the Beautiful River. The 4th, in the morning, having conferred with Messrs. the officers, and the principal Indians of my detachment upon the precautions to be taken for reassuring the nations of the Beautiful River, and to induce them not to flee, so that we could speak to them on the part of M. the Governor, it was decided that M. de Joncaire should go with the chiefs to the village of Attique to announce my arrival there and induce the nations of that place to await me without fear, since I came only to speak of good things. He immediately set out. We made about fifteen leagues that day.

The 5th I set out at a pretty early hour. After having made from three to four leagues I found a river, the mouth of which is very beautiful, and at a league lower-down I found another. Both of them are to the south of the Beautiful River. On the highground there are villages of the Loups and Iroquois of the Five Nations. I camped at an early hour in order to give M. de Joncaire time to reach the village of Attique. The 6th I set out about seven o'clock. After having made about five leagues I arrived at the village of Attique,[41] where I found M. de Joncaire with our Indians. Those of the place had taken flight. This village consists of twenty-two cabins. They are Loups. M. de Joncaire told me that a chief with two young men who had remained to spy, seeing him meagerly accompanied, had come to him and demanded of him the motives of his voyage; to which he answered: I come only to speak to the nations of the Beautiful River, to animate the children of the (French) government which inhabited it. He induced this chief to take charge of the wampum belts, which I had given him, to carry them to the villages lower down, and to tell them to remain quiet upon their mats, since I only came to treat of affairs with them, which would be advantageous to them. I re-embarked and the same day I passed by the ancient village of the Chauenons,[42] which has been abandoned since the departure of an individual named Chartier, and his band, who was taken away from this place by the orders of M. the Marquis of Beauharnois,[43] and conducted to the River au Vermillion, on the Wabash, in 1745. At this place I fell in with six English soldiers, with fifty horses and about one hundred and fifty bales of furs, who were returning from there to Philadelphia. I summoned them in writing to withdraw to their own territory, that the land whither they had come on business belonged to the King (of France), and not to the King of England, that if they came again they would be pillaged; that I desired this time to treat them with kindness, and that they should profit of the advice I gave them. They assured me, either through fear or otherwise, that they would not come back any more. They acknowledged that they had no right to trade, a point which I had explained clearly in the citation. I wrote to the Governor of Philadelphia in these terms :

Sir.--Having been sent with a detachment into these parts by the orders of M. the Marquis de La Galissonière, Governor-General of New France, in order to reconcile with it some Indian nations which had fallen away on the occasion of the war that is just ended.[44] I have been very much surprised to find some merchants of your, government in this country, to which England has never had any pretensions. I have treated them with all possible mildness, though I had a right to look upon them as intruders and mere vagrants, their traffic being contrary to the preliminaries of the peace, signed more than fifteen months ago.

I hope, Sir, you will condescend to forbid this trade for the future, which is contrary to the treaties; and that you will warn your traders not to return into these territories; for, if so, they can only impute to themselves the evils which might befall them. I know that our Governor-General would be very sorry to have to resort to violent measures, but he has received positive orders not to allow foreign merchants or traders in his government. I am, etc.

This done, I re-embarked and continued my route. The 7th I passed by a Loup village in which there were only three men. They had placed a white flag[45] over their cabins, the rest of their people had gone to Chiningue, not hazarding to remain at home. I invited these three men to come along with me to Chiningue in order to hear what I had to say to them. I re-embarked and went to the village which is called the Written Rock. They are Iroquois that inhabit this place, and it was an old woman[46] of that nation, who led the them. She looks upon herself as queen and is entirely devoted to the English. All the Indians withdrew; there remained in this place only six English traders, who came all trembling before me. I landed, and when I wished to speak to them I was much embarrassed, not having an interpreter of their language, and they pretended not to understand others. However, they yielded, and one among them spoke Chavenoun.[47] I made the same citation to them as to the others, and I wrote to their Governor. They told me they were going to withdraw, that they knew well they had no right to trade, but not having encountered any obstacles up to the present, they had sought to gain their livelihood; and the more so as the Indians had attracted them thither, but that henceforward they would not return. This place is one of the most beautiful I have seen up to the present on the Beautiful River. I decamped and passed the night about three leagues lower down. When we had landed our Indians told me that when passing they had seen certain writings on a rock. As it was late I could not send anyone there till the next day. I begged the Reverend Father Bonnecamps and M. de Joncaire to go there in the hope that these writings might: afford me some light. They set out early in the morning and brought me back word that they were nothing more than some English names written with charcoal. As I was only two leagues from Chiningue[48] I made the men of my detachment brush themselves up as well as possible, so as to give them a better appearance, and I arranged everything for repairing to the village in good order, as I considered this one of the most considerable villages of the Beautiful River. The 8th, as I was preparing to embark, I saw a canoe come in sight with two men. I judged they were persons sent from the village, so I awaited them. They were only men who came expressly to examine by my countenance if they could discover my plans. I received them with kindness and had them drink a cup of the milk of their father Onontio. Among the Indian nations this is always the greatest mark of friendship that one can make them. After having conversed some time they asked me to let them go back to their villages, and begged me to give them about an hour in advance so that they might prepare themselves to receive me. Shortly after their departure I embarked, after having examined my men's arms, and having ammunition distributed in case of need; and having to take many precautions with nations frightened and mad, I ordered that there should be only four guns charged with powder to each canoe, to answer the salutes, and eight loaded with bullets; when I was in sight of the village I discovered three French and one English flag; as soon as I was descried salutes of musketry were fired from the village, and, as the current is extremely strong at this part of the shallow river, there came an Iroquois in front of me to point out the channel. I was brought there in an instant by the swiftness of the current. When landing they fired a discharge of balls for us. This sort of salute is given by all the nations of the south, and accidents frequently occur from it. This manner of saluting did not surprise me more than it did the officers of my detachment, still, as I had suspicions of them, and had no confidence in their good intentions, I had M. de Joncaire tell them to stop firing in this manner or I would open fire on them. I had them ordered at the same time to knock down the English tent, or I would have it taken away myself. This was done immediately, a woman cut the pole and the flag has not been seen since. I landed, and, as the strand is extremely narrow, and disadvantageous in case the Indians had bad intentions, it being at the bottom of a slope thirty feet or more in height, I had to place myself as advantageously as those who might be make an attack. I fixed my camp securely near the village and made it appear as strong as it was possible for me. I had body guards placed on the right and the left, I ordered sentinels to be placed at a short distance from each other, and bivouacked for the night. Messrs. the officers who were not on guard received orders to make the night rounds. These precautions prevented the Indians from executing what they had planned, and which M. de Joncaire found out a short time afterwards through the means of some woman of his acquaintance. This village consists of fifty cabins, composed of Iroquois, Channanous, Loups and a part of the men of the villages I had passed, who had come to seek refuge there, and to render them stronger. About five o'clock in the evening the Chiefs, accompanied by thirty or forty braves, came to salute me. They complimented me on my arrival at their place. The following is the opening discourse of the 8th of August, 1749

Two belts of wampum.

"My father, by these two belts of wampum we come to testify to you the joy we have to see you arrive in our village in good health. We thank the master of Life for having preserved you on a route so long and so difficult as that which you have made. It is a long while since we have had the satisfaction of seeing the French in our village. We behold you here, my father, with pleasure. You must have noticed by the flag which you have seen in our village that our heart is entirely French. The young men, without perceiving the consequences, erected the one which displeased you. As soon we knew it you saw it fall. It was only put up for show, and to divert the young folks, without once thinking that the matter would have displeased you. We invite you also, my father, by these wampum belts, to open your heart to us and show us what can have displeased you. We believe that you came to speak to us on the part of our father Onontio. We are ready to hear his word, and we pray you to condescend to remain until the chiefs of the village, whom we are awaiting, shall have arrived."

41

Answer of M. de Celoron:

Two belts of wampum.

"I am grateful to you, my children, for the pleasure which you appear to have at seeing me arrive in your village. I have only come here, as you see, on the part of your father Onontio, to speak of good things. It is this which I shall explain to you tomorrow, when you will be all assembled. You are right in saying that the English flag which I perceived over your village displeased me. This mingling of French and English does not become the children of the Governor, and would seem to indicate that their hearts are divided. Let it be broken down in such a manner as to be never raised again. The young men have erected it without prudence, the old men have taken it away with reflection, and they have done well. By these two belts of wampum I, in my turn, open your ears and your eyes in order that you may hear well tomorrow what I have to say to you on the part of your father Onontio."

They retired, and in order to have themselves ready for any occurrence, they passed the night dancing, keeping, however, their men on the alert. The 9th, before daybreak, M. de Joncaire, whom I had charged, as well as M. his brother, to watch during the night the maneuvers of the Indians, came to tell me that he had been notified that eighty braves were on the point of arriving, and that the resolution to attack us had been taken in the village. On hearing this, which I communicated to Messrs. the officers, I gave new orders so that all might be ready in case we should have to come to close quarters. I had all my men keep themselves in readiness. I placed Messrs. the officers in such positions that they could assist and encourage each other to perform their duty well, and I waited two hours to see how the resolution of the Indians would be carried out. Seeing that nothing was attempted, I despatched M. de Joncaire to tell them that I knew the resolution they had taken, and awaited them with impatience; and if they did not make haste and put in execution what they had planned, I would go and attack them. A short time after the return of M. de Joncaire, the Indians filed before my camp and made the accustomed salute. They may have numbered about fifty men, according to what was told me by several officers who had counted them as they filed by. Many braves of the village had arrived earlier during the night.

About two hours after the arrival of these braves, the principal men with those of the village came to my tent with pipes of peace to offer me their compliments and to present them to me to smoke. Before accepting them I rebuked them for their manner of acting, in terms which were thoroughly explained to them by Monsieur de Joncaire. The following is the discourse I addressed to them:

Discourse of M. de Celoron to the Indians of Chiningue, with four belts of wampum, the 9th of August, 1749:

"I am surprised, my children, that (after having the condescension to send Monsieur de Joncaire to the Village of the Cut Straw and Attique to announce to you my arrival in this part of the country, and to let you know that I bringing the word of your father Onontio.) to see you frightened, abashed, and making manoeuvres which at no time were becoming for the children of the governor. I informed you by these belts of wampum that I came only to do good; they have been sent you; you should, then, believe me. You are well enough acquainted with the Frenchman to know that he is sincere, and never speaks from the lips only. If I ever had such designs as you imagine, or such as the evil-minded have told you, I would have concealed my expedition from you, as that was easy for me to do, and I would not have arrived so peaceably at your village as I have done. I know how to make war, and those who have made war with us ought to know it, too, so I cannot act the part of a deceiver. By these four belts of wampum I again open your ears, I enlighten your minds and I take away the bandage which you have over your eyes, so that you may be able to hear the word of your father Onontio, who is filled with kindness towards you, though he has had reason to be dissatisfied with some among you. Now I desire heartily to smoke your pipes to prove to you that I have forgotten all you have done. I shall speak to you to-morrow on the part of your father Onontio; I invite you to drive away the bad spirit which seduces you and which will inevitably ruin you if you do not pay attention."

I smoked the pipes, and they went away well pleased, and remained quiet the rest of the day and the following night. The 10th of August, about ten in the morning, I made the chiefs and a part of the braves assemble in my camp. I had a place prepared for the council, and I told

43

them the word of M. the Governor, to which they listened with marked attention.

Message of Monsieur the Marquis de La Galissonière to the nations of Chiningue brought by Monsieur de Celoron, the 10th of August. 1749, A belt.

"The friendship which I entertain for you, my children, despite your estrangement from me, has induced me to send you Monsieur de Celoron to bring you a message and induce you`to open your eyes with regard to the projects which the English form on your territories. Undoubtedly you are not aware of the establishments which they propose making thereon, which tend to nothing short of your total ruin. They hide from you their idea of establishing themselves therein in such a way as to render themselves masters of that territory, and drive you away, if I should let them do so. I ought, then, like a good father who loves his children tenderly, and who, though far away from them, bears them all in his heart, to apprise them of the danger that threatens them, which is the design that the English have formed to take possession of your territories, and to succeed in that they have begun to bias your minds. You know, my children, that they have left nothing undone during the last war to turn you against me, but the greater part of your nation have had courage enough not to listen to them. I feel grateful to these, and. like a kind father, I forget the past, persuaded that, for the future, you will remain quiet in your own territories, no matter what wars I may have with the English. It is to your own advantage to observe the neutrality which you yourselves asked of me when you came to Montreal; to which demand I deigned to consent, and by this means you will preserve this peace which constitutes the happiness of the nations. As I know the English only inspire you with evil sentiments, and, besides, intend, through their establishments on the Beautiful River, which belongs to me, to take it from me, I have summoned them to retire, and I have the greater right for so doing from the fact that it has been stipulated between the Kings of France and England, that the English should never repair thither for trade or aught else. It is even one of the conditions of the peace which we have just made together. Moreover, the Chiefs of the Five Nations have told them not to pass over the mountains which form their boundaries. I do not wish to employ violence this time with regard to the English. I shall tell them quietly my determination that they should pay attention; for, if afterwards misfortunes befall them, they can only blame themselves. For you, my children, rest on your mats and do not enter into the disputes I may have with the English. I will take care for all that may be for your advantage, I invite you to come to see me next year. I will give you marks of my friendship and will put you in such a condition as not to regret those whom I advise you not to suffer among you. I will give you all the assistance of a kind father who loves you, and who will let you want for nothing. Those whom we shall bring to you will never covet your territories. either by purchase or usurpation; on the contrary, I will order them to maintain you thereon in spite of all opposition, and your interests shall be common with mine, if you behave well. By this means you will be always tranquil and peace will reign in your villages. I would, my children, tell you the sentiments of your father before speaking to the English, whom I am going to look for to tell them to retire."

The counsel finished, they appeared well pleased with what I had told them, and went to their villages to prepare their answer, which I told them to do for the next day, having a long way to go, and the season being far advanced. This village is composed of Iroquois, Chanavaus and of Loups, for which cause the council lasted for more than four hours. Besides these three nations there are in this village Iroquois from the Sault St. Louis, from the Lake of the Two Mountains, and Indians from the Nepisiniques[49] and the Abenakis, with Ontarios[50] and other nations. This gathering forms a bad village, which is seduced by the allurements of cheap merchandise furnished by the English, which keeps them in very bad disposition towards us. I had the most prominent of the English merchants called to me, to whom I addressed a summons to retire into their own territory with all their servants, just as I had done with regard to those whom I had previously met. They answered like the others, that they would do so, that they knew well they had no right to trade on the Beautiful River. I added that their government was bounded by the mountains, and that they should not pass beyond what was agreed to. I wrote to the Governor of Carolina in terms similar to those I had employed in writing to the Governor at Philadelphia.

The 11th of August, the Indians came to give me their answers. If they are sincere, I believe Monsieur the Governor-General will be satisfied with them; but there is little reliance to be placed on the promise of such people, and the more so, as I have just said, since their personal interests make them look with favorable eyes on the English, who give them their merchandise at one-fourth the price; hence there is reason to think the King of England or the country makes up the loss which the merchants sustain in their sales to draw the nations to them. It is true that the expenses of the English are not near so considerable as those which our merchants would be obliged to contract on account of the difficulty of the route. It is, however, certain that we can never regain the nations, except by furnishing them merchandise at the same price as the English; the difficulty is to find out the means?

These are the answers which the Indians of Chiningue made to the message of M. the Governor-General, the 11th of August, 1749:

"My father, we are very glad to see you to-day, and (are pleased) with the manner in which you regard us. The Commanders of Detroit and Niagara had told us to go see Onontio; to-day you come yourself to invite us to go down. One must be insane not to pay attention to your word. By this string we assure you that all the nations who inhabit this river will go down next spring to hear the word of our father Onontio. Nothing will be able to turn us away from the sentiments which we now entertain. Even though but one person should remain, he will have the pleasure of seeing our father. The shoes which we wear at the thawing of the ice would not be able to carry us to Montreal we pray him to make provision on that score so that we may find some at Niagara when we are passing that way. My father, have pity on us, we have no longer any ancient chiefs; it is only young people that now speak to you. Pardon the faults which we may commit because you, who are wisdom itself, also make some. You have expelled the English from this territory, and to this we heartily agree; but you ought to bring with you traders to furnish us with what we need. If you have pity for us, let us have the English so that they may render us the assistance which is necessary until spring-time. You see in what an unfortunate plight we shall be, if you do not show us this kindness. Do not be surprised at not finding answers to your belts. Those you behold here are only young men who keep their pipes; When our chiefs and our braves return, we shall intimate to them your intentions, and the sentiments of our father Onontio; and, in order that we may be at ease we pray you to leave with us one of your children, Joncaire, to conduct us to our father and assist us."

Answer of Monsieur de Celoron to the demand which the Indians made of him, to have one of the Messrs. Joncaire:

"My children, it is not in my power to dispose of any of the officers which your father has confided to me. When you go down you can ask him one of the Messrs. Joncaire, and I am convinced he will not refuse him to you."

Continuation of the reply of the Indians:

"We thank you for the hope which you give us that our father will grant us one of your children. We again assure you that we will do, without reserve, all that you have asked of us. We would be glad to be able to see you longer, and we thank our brethren who are along with you for the advice they have given us, and we shall pay attention to it."

When the Council was finished I had the presents brought forward that I had destined for them. They were considerable enough. They were much flattered by them. I encouraged them anew to hold to what they had I promised me, and above all to come to see Monsieur the Governor-General next year, assuring them that they would have reason to be well pleased with their reception at the hands of their father Onontio. My business finished, I had my canoes launched and embarked to continue my voyage. About four leagues lower down there is a river to the south on which there are several villages. I did not land there, having spoken to them at Chiningue.

I embarked about six in the morning. Having made from four or five leagues I fell in with two pirogues laden with packages and manned by four Englishmen. All that I could get out of them was, that they were coming from St. Yotoc,[51] whence they had set out twenty-five days previous. I had no English interpreters, and they did not know how to speak French or Iroquois, which was the only language of which I had an interpreter. I re-embarked and continued my route until three o'clock, and having many sick I made my Indians go a hunting in hope that this Beautiful River, which had been reported to Monsieur the Governor-General as abounding in buffaloes, might furnish some to regale my men who were living on nothing but sea biscuit. But I was disappointed, my Indians killed nothing but a few deer which was a poor comfort to hungry and infirm persons.

The 13th I set out early in the morning and fell in with several pirogues manned by Iroquois who were going to hunt among those rivers which flow from the territories. At noon I made a halt, and had a leaden plate buried at the entrance of the River Kanonuara,[52] to the south of the Beautiful River, and had the arms of the King attached to a tree, and drew up the following official statement of it.

Official statement of the depositing of a leaden plate at the mouth of the River Kanonuara.

The year 1749, we, Celoron, Knight of the Royal and Military Order of St. Louis, and Captain commanding a detachment sent by the orders of Monsieur the Marquis de la Galissonière, Governor-General of Canada, upon the Beautiful River, accompanied by the principal officers of our detachment, have buried at the foot of a large elm tree at the entrance of the river and upon the southern bank of the Kanonuara, which empties itself at the east of the river Oyo, a leaden plate, and have attached to a tree in the same spot, the arms of the King. In testimony whereof we have drawn up and signed, along with Messrs. the officers, the present official statement, at our camp, the 13th of August, 1749.

The 14th I set out at 7 o'clock, not being able to do so sooner on account of the fog. I passed two rivers, the mouths of which are very beautiful. The hunting was very fair that day in deer. The 15th I continued my voyage and buried a leaden plate at the mouth of the river Jenuanguekouan,[53] and drew up the following official statement of it:

Official statement of the depositing of a fourth leaden plate at the entrance of the river Jenuanguekouan, the 15th of August, 1749:

The 15th of August, 1749, we, Celoron, Knight of the Royal and Military Order of St. Louis, Captain commanding a detachment sent by the orders of Monsieur the Marquis de la Galissonière, Governor-General of Canada, upon the Beautiful River, otherwise called the River Oyo, accompanied by the principal officers of our detachment, have buried at the foot of a maple tree, which forms a triangle with a red oak and an elm tree, at the entrance of the river Jenuanguekouan, at the western bank of that river, a leaden plate, and have attached to a tree on the spot, the arms of the King. In testimony whereof we have drawn up and signed

48

the present official statement, along with Messrs. the officers at our camp, the 15th of August, 1749.

The 16th I could not get off before nine o'clock, having out several hunters, both French and Indians, who had passed the night in the woods. I made about twelve leagues. The 17th I embarked about seven o'clock. In the course of the day I passed two beautiful rivers, which flowed down from the lands, the one to the north, the other to the south of the Beautiful River, the names of which I do not know. I landed early for the sake of a hunt, for all were reduced to the biscuit. The 18th I set out at a pretty early hour, I encamped at noon as the rain hindered us from continuing our voyage. That same day I deposited a leaden plate at the entrance of the river Chinodaista,[54] and had the arms of the King attached to a tree. This river bears canoes for forty leagues without meeting rapids, and takes its rise near Carolina. The English of that government come that way to ply their trade on the Beautiful River.
Official statement of the fifth leaden plate, placed at the entrance of the river Chinodaista, the 18th of August, 1749:

The year 1749, we, Celoron, Knight of the Royal and Military Order of St. Louis, Captain commanding a detachment sent by the orders of Monsieur the Marquis de la Galissonière, Governor-General of Canada: upon the Beautiful River, otherwise called L'oyo, accompanied by the principal officers of our detachment, have buried at the foot of an elm tree, upon the southern bank of the Loyo, and the eastern bank Chinodaista, a leaden plate, and have attached to a tree in the same spot the arms of the King. In testimony whereof, we have drawn up the present official statement, and which we have signed along with Messrs. the officers at Our camp, the 18th of August, 1749.

The 19th the rain continued so violently that I was forced to pitch my camp on higher grounds, the bottom lands being inundated. The 20th I re-embarked and after making a few leagues, seeing a man standing on the bottom lands I went to him; it was a Loup Indian who was returning from a war waged on the Chien Nation.[55] It was sixteen days since he had set out alone without food or ammunition. I gave him as much as would enable him to reach Chiningue, from which he was still far distant. I questioned him with regard to the number of people there might be at St.

Yotoc. He answered me that there might he about 80 cabins there, and perhaps 100. I continued my voyage till three o'clock, and then made my men go hunting. The 21st the Indians of my detachment came looking for me to represent to me that they were afraid to go to St. Yotoc without having previously given notice to the nations of that place of my designs, because this was a considerable village, and there was reason to fear that these Indians were apprised of my voyage and would be restless from the fact that those who had brought them the news of my arrival might, as in the case of the villages by which I had passed, have carried them false reports, which would lead them to lay ambushes for us. When drawing near the village I assembled the officers to discuss the part we should take. It was arranged that we should despatch a canoe to St. Yotoc to pacify the natives and rouse their courage in case some news-mongers might have caused them trouble. It was Monsieur de Joncaire that I appointed to go there along with Ceganeis-Kassin and Saetaguinrale, two chiefs from the Sault St. Louis, faithful servants of the King, and three Abenaki chiefs. Monsieur de Minerville[56] asked permission to go there too, and I let him. I gave those sent some hours of advance. Then I embarked about 7 o'clock in the morning, after having distributed war ammunition to all my men, and encouraged them to act their part well in case the Indians wished to attack us. After making about four leagues I discovered a canoe, armed by from seven to eight men, and which had a white flag. As soon is they perceived me they landed and I went to them. It was Monsieur de Joncaire with seven Indians, both Chanenoies and Iroquois. As soon as I landed the chief came and shook hands with me. The others did the same, and kept silent for some time. These men seemed to me to be much disturbed, I asked the reason of this circumstance of Monsieur de Joncaire, and he told me that the nations of St. Yotoc were frightened out of their wits, and that when they perceived himself and his companions drawing near, they fired balls on them and even pierced their flag with three bullets; that on landing they were conducted to the council cabin, and when they would explain the subject of their commission an Indian arose and interrupted them, saying that the French deceived them, and that they came only to destroy them and their families; that at that instant the young men had rushed to arms, saying that these Frenchmen should be killed, and that after they had dispatched their own families to the woods, they should then go and lay ambushes for the canoes. According to what Monsieur and the Indians who were in his company told me, all this would have been carried into execution by them, were it not for an Iroquois chief who averted the storm, pacified them and volunteered to come to me along with any others who were disposed to follow him; and, for security, they retain M. de Minerville and the Indians. Finally, after a silence of a half-hour's duration, the Iroquois chief arose and said to me:

"My father, you behold before you young men without intelligence, who were on the point of embroiling the land in turmoil forever. Look on us in pity and show no resentment for what we have done. When you arrive at our village our old men will testify their sorrow for the fault they have committed. For the last two months we have been like drunken men, by reason of the false reports which were brought to us by the villages through which you have passed."

I answered him thus:

"I do not know what you wish to say to me when I shall have arrived at St. Yotoc. I shall make inquiry and see what I shall have to do. I know you have come to meet me with good dispositions. You would have done wisely in bringing back the Indians who were with M. de Joncaire. You may go back to your village, I will go there in a little time. You will give notice to the young men that they must dispense with saluting me according to their custom."

I gave him and those along with him a drink and sent them away, for M. de Joncaire said to me: "I knew right well that these Indians were badly disposed and much frightened, since in the space of twice twenty-four hours they had constructed a stone fort, strongly built and in good condition for their defense." This caused me to make the most serious reflections. I was aware of the weakness of my detachment; two-thirds were recruits who had never made an attack, and who, on first seeing the Indians of my detachment, had taken flight. It was not in my power to choose others, and notwithstanding the recommendations made by M. the Marquis de La Galissonière when setting out for Quebec, to give me picked men, they paid no regard to them there. In fine, there was no other course left me to pursue than to continue my voyage without provisions, having my canoes unfit for service, without pitch or bark. I re-embarked, prepared for whatever might happen. I had excellent officers and about fifty men on whom I could rely. At a quarter-of-a-league's distance from the village I was descried. The salutes began immediately, and those Indians discharged well nigh a thousand gunshots. I knew the powder had been gratuitously furnished them by the English. I landed opposite to the village and had a return salute fired. The chiefs and the old men crossed the river and came to me with flags and pipes of peace; they had the grass cut in order to make seats for us. and invited me to sit down along with the officers. They led back with them Sieur de Minerville and the Indians whom they had retained. As we were about sitting down about 80 men crossed over, armed and accoutred as warriors. I ordered my detachment under arms. These 80 men lined a hedge about twenty paces from us, and leaned on their guns. I told the chief that I was astonished at the manoeuvres of these harebrained creatures, and that if they did not move out of that immediately I would fire upon them. He answered me that they did not come with any bad intention, but merely to salute us again, and that they should retire since it displeased me. This they did immediately, firing their guns in the air, which were only loaded with blank cartridges. Pipes were then presented to me and to all the officers. After this ceremony a Chaouenous chief arose and complimented me upon my arrival. I told them that I would speak to them tomorrow in my tent where I would light the Governor's fire. They answered me that they had in their village a council cabin where they would hear me, if I repaired thither with all my officers, with regard to what I had to say to them on the part of their father Onontio. I refused their demand, and said it was their place to come to me to hear what I had to say to them. They being much displeased it would have been a great imprudence to go to their village, so I held firm to this point and brought them round to my views. They returned to their village. We posted guards, and the rounds were kept up during the whole night very scrupulously by the officers. It is to be remarked that since the inhabitants of this village composed for the most part of Chavenois and Iroquois of the Five Nations, there were added more than thirty men from the Sault St. Louis, waste had destroyed the abundance of game, the cheap merchandise which the English furnished was very seducing motives for them to remain attached to the latter. The son of Arteganukassin is there, and neither his father nor myself could succeed in taking him away. Besides the men from the Sault St. Louis, there are also some from the lake of the Two Mountains, some Loups from the Miami, and nearly all the nations from the territory of Enhault. All these taken together were no better than Chavenois, who are entirely devoted to the English. The 23d I sent them word by Monsieur de Joncaire to come to my camp to hear the words of their father. At first they refused to come, saying that it was in the council cabin they should be spoken to. I answered by saying that it was the duty of children to come and find their father where he wished to light his fire. After some parleying they came to my camp and make their excuse in these terms:

Speech of the Indians of St. Yotoc to M. de Celoron, with four belts of wampum, the 23d of August, 1749:

"My father, we are ashamed to appear before you after the excesses we committed yesterday with regard to those whom you sent us. We are in despair, we ask pardon of you for it, and of our brethren, and we beseech you to forget this great mistake. The sorrow we feel for it gives us hope that you will pardon us."

Answer of Monsieur de Celoron to the Indians of St. Yotoc, the same day.

"My children, no one could be more astonished than I was when I learned by the canoe which came to me, the reception which you had given to the chiefs whom I sent to you, to announce my arrival, and to tell you that I came to bring you the word of your father Onontio. They had gone to quiet you with all the signs capable of proving to you that I only came to your village in a peaceful manner. This sign so honourable for all the other tribes was not so for you; so you fired on them; and not content with that, you have shown more deference for the word of a wicked man, who is a hypocrite, than you did for mine. I was more surprised, since believing for a long time that the Chavenous were men of courage, they have showed themselves too smart on this occasion in insulting those who were to send them. What has then become of that good spirit, Chavenous, which you had, when, ten years ago, Monsieur de Longueil passed by here on his way to the Chuachias.[57] You came out to meet him, and you showed him in every way the kindness of your hearts. A company of young men also volunteered to accompany him, yet he did not give you notice of his coming. But at that time you had a

French heart, and today you let it be corrupted by the English who dwell among you continually and who, under pretext of ministering to your wants, seek only to ruin you. Reflect on these just rebukes I am making you, and have no confidence in those bad people who will turn out, if you do not be on your guard, the ruin off your nation.

"With four belts of wampum you stuffed my throat on my arrival. I had no need of this sort of medicine. The heart of the Governor is always kind towards his children, but as you stand in need of a stronger proof than this, by these belts of wampum I dispel all your evil dispositions. The pardon which you solicit for your fault, and the sorrow which you seem to have for it, constrain me to pardon you. Be wiser for the future. As you ask me, I bury this unhappy affair, and I will ask your father Onontio, not to keep any remembrance of it. I invite you to reject all the deceitful talk which may be addressed to you, and I invite you in future to hear well the speech of your father Onontio, which I bring to you."

Speech of M. the General to the Indians of the village of St. Yotoc, brought by M. de Celoron with a belt, the 23d August, 1749:

"My children, the friendship I entertain for you, although far away, has induced me to send M. de Celoron to open your eyes and disclose to you the projects which the English are forming in your regard, and that of the territories also which you inhabit. Undoubtedly you are not aware of the establishments that they are thinking of making there which tend to nothing short of your ruin. They conceal from you their idea, which is to build on your territories forts sufficiently strong to destroy you, if I would allow them to do so. I ought then as a kind father who loves his children tenderly, and who, though far away from them, always thinks of their good, to give them notice of the danger which threatens them. You know, my children, that they omitted nothing in the last war I had with them to induce you to declare against me. Happy for you that you did not listen to them, and I am thankful to you for it. Others let themselves be drawn away, I have pardoned some of them, persuaded that they will be more prudent for the future, and will no more listen to these evil spirits who seek only to trouble the land. But to shield you completely from their seduction I have sent to summon them to withdraw immediately from off my territories wherein they never had a right to enter, the kings of France and England having agreed in the treaties of peace, that the

English should never come for trade or aught else upon the Beautiful River. I did not wish to employ force on this occasion; though I had the right to have them pillaged, I notified them peacefully to pay attention; if another time misfortune befall them, they have only themselves to blame. For you, my children, remain quiet in your wigwams and do enter into the contentions I may have with the English; I will take care for all that may be for your advantage. I invite you to come see me next year, I shall then give you marks of my friendship, and shall put you in such a state as not to regret those whom I remove from my territories. I shall afford you all the assistance which you have a right to look for from a kind father who loves you and will not let you want for anything. Those who will bring you this assistance, will not invade your lands nor drive you away from them; on the contrary, I have given them orders to maintain you therein, and your interests and mine shall always be the same.

A belt.

"For the two years that 1 have been in the country I have been entirely taken up in finding out the interests of my children, and all that could be of advantage to them. I have learned with regret the affair which transpired between you and the Illinois;[58] as you are equally my children and I have the heart of a father for you, I charge M. de Celoron whom I send into the villages of the Beautiful River, to carry my speech, and to present you with this belt on my part in order to induce you to become reconciled with your brethren the Illinois. I have taken the same steps with them, having despatched to the commander of that post[59] an order to speak with them on my part, and to tell them to remain quiet. I hope, my children, that you, one and all, will hear my speech with pleasure, and that you will strive to live in peace and harmony as my real and true children. I do not enter into the subject of your quarrel, I am even ignorant as to who is the aggressor; but no matter how that may be, it is his place to make the necessary advances for a reconciliation, and the offended party should forget the injury received. I shall be much obliged to them for so doing, and the more so as I seek only to procure them that which is most advantageous."

Whilst we were in council a Chanenous entered with a very frightened look and told the chief that all the nations of Detroit (or the narrows) were coming to fall upon them, and that whilst I was amusing them, they were going to see their villages destroyed. I saw that the Indians were excited; I asked the cause of it, and having learned it, I calmed their fear and so encouraged them that the council was interrupted but for a short time. After having explained to them the intentions of M. the General, I gave them a cup to drink. They went back to their village. As soon as they were gone, I sent M. de Joncaire to get information with regard to the news that had just arrived. It was not long till he came back and reported to me that it was three Ontarios who had arrived at a village in the territory at a distance of ten leagues from St. Yotoc, and that couriers had set out immediately to bring us the news; that the Ontarios would not arrive for two days. I conjectured that they were the couriers that M. de Sabrinois sent me to give me notice of the dispositions of the people of Detroit.

The 24th. The Indians hesitated, after having raised some difficulties, to come and give their answer in the French camp, but seeing that I persisted with firmness in my manner, they came, and here is their answer very badly explained, their interpreter being very ignorant.

Answer of the Indians of St. Yotoc, to the speech of M. the General, the 24th of August, 1749, with six belts of wampum:

"My father, we come to tell you that we have listened to the speech of our father Onontio, with great pleasure, that all he has told to us is true and intended for our good, and that we ourselves and our brethren who are here present will conform to it, having but one and the same mind. By these belts of wampum we assure our father Onontio, that all who dwell in our village will no more play an evil part and will no longer listen to bad talk. My father, we render you our thanks for wishing to reconcile us with our brethren, the Illinois. We promise you to labor at bringing this about. That speech has afforded much pleasure to our entire village. My father, by these belts of wampum we thank you for the manner in which you have spoken to us; we encourage you to continue your route, and to animate all your children, so that the land may be at peace for us Chananaous, and we assure you that we shall labor henceforth only in what is right."

The 25th, I had all the chiefs assemble, and bestowed on them a present on the part of M. the General, and urged them to keep the promise they had given me. A little while after I summoned the English traders to appear and commanded them to withdraw, making them feel that they had no right to trade or aught else on the Beautiful River. I wrote to the Governor of Carolina, whom I fully apprised of the danger his traders would expose themselves to, if they returned there. I was ordered to do this in my instructions, and even to plunder the English, but I was not strong enough for that, the traders having established themselves in the village and being well sustained by the Indians, I would he only undertaking a task which would not have succeeded, and which would only have redounded to the disgrace of the French. The Ontarios, sent by M. de Sabrinois, arrived and brought me two letters in which he informed me that there was nothing in what M. La Naudiere had told me with regard to the dispositions of the Indians of Detroit; that it was rather the contrary; for notwithstanding several efforts made by M. Longueuil and himself to urge them to march, they had constantly refused. I gave the couriers some provisions, which were at present very much stinted, and I wrote to M. de Sabrinois and besought him to keep twenty canoes in reserve for me at the foot of the narrows, with provisions for my detachment, against the beginning of October.

The 26th. I set out at ten in the morning from St. Yotoc; all the Indians were under arms and fired a salute when I passed before the village. The 27th of August I arrived at the White River[60] about six in the evening. I knew that at a distance of three leagues in the country there were cabins of my friends, and that influenced me to pass the night in this place. The 28th, I sent M. Devillier and my son[61] to these cabins in order to tell those Indians to come and speak with me. They brought them back with them, and I induced them to come with me to the village of the Demoiselle,[62] whither I was going to bring the word of their father Onontio. They gave their consent and asked (to be permitted) to remain till the next day in order to have time to prepare for the journey. There are in this village two cabins of Sonontouans. It is the policy of these nations to have always along with them some (other Indians) who serve as a hostage. I induced one of these Sonontouans who spake Miami very well, to come with me to the Demoiselle, for I had need of him, having no interpreter, though I had to treat with these people on matters of importance.

The 29th. I wrote to M. Raimond,[63] captain and commander among the Miamis, and besought him to send me the so-called royal interpreter with as many horses as he possibly could, to transport our baggage over a portage of fifty leagues. The 30th the Indians of the White River having arrived, I embarked to gain the Rock River,[64] and at the entrance I had a leaden plate buried, and the arms of the King attached to a tree, of which I drew up an official statement.

Official statement of the sixth leaden plate buried at the entrance of the Rock River, the 31st day of August, 1749.

The year 1749, we, Celoron, Knight of the Royal and Military Order of St. Louis, Captain, commanding a detachment sent by the orders of M. the Marquis de la Galissonière, Governor-General of Canada, upon the Beautiful River, otherwise called the Ohio, accompanied by the principal officers of our detachment, have buried at the point formed by the right bank of the Ohio and the left bank of Rock River, a leaden plate, and have attached to a tree the arms of the King. In testimony whereof, we have drawn up and signed with Messrs. the officers, the present official statement.

The inscription is always the same.

7th September. This done, I embarked; owing to the scarcity of water in this river, it took thirteen days in ascending it. The 12th. The Miamis of the village of the Demoiselle having learned that I was on the point of arriving among them, sent four chiefs to meet me with pipes of peace to have me smoke; as the half of my people were on land, there not being water enough in the river to float the freighted canoes. I was informed by M. de Courtemanche,[65] the officer of the detachment, of the arrival of his messengers, I landed at the place where they were, and when we were all seated they began the ceremony of presenting the pipe. I accepted it. They then brought it to M. de Contrecoeur, second captain of the detachment, and to all the officers and the Canadians, who, worn out for a smoke, would have wished that the ceremony had continued longer. The hour having come for camping, we passed the night in this place. The messengers remaining with us, I was obliged, despite the scarcity of provisions then in my possession to give them supper.

The 13th. I arrived at the village of the Demoiselle. I pitched my camp, placed my sentinels, and awaited the arrival of the interpreter I had asked of M. de Raimond. During this interval, I sounded their minds in order to learn if they were disposed to return to Kiskakon, for that is the name of their ancient village. It seemed to me that they had not much objection. They had two English soldiers in their village whom I obliged to go away before speaking to these people. Those who had spent the summer there trading, had already departed overland with their effects; they had ways of communication from one village to another.

The 17th. Wearied at the fact of the interpreter not arriving, and because my provisions were being consumed while thus waiting, I determined to speak to the Demoiselle by means of an Iroquois who knew Miami well. I showed them magnificent presents on the part of M. the General to induce them to return to their villages, and I explained to them his invitations in these terms:

Speech of M. the General to the Miamis of the band of the Demoiselle, established at Rock River, and at the Baril located at the White River, brought by M. de Celoron, 17th of September, 1749, with eight belts of wampum for the two villages:

"My children: The manner in which I behave toward you, despite all you have done to the French whom I sent you to maintain your wives and your children, ought to be a sufficient proof of the attachment which I have for you and the sincerity of my feelings. I forget what you have done to me, and I bury it in the depth of the earth in order to never more remember it, convinced that you have acted only at the instigation of a people whose policy is to trouble the land and destroy the good disposition of those with whom they have relations, and who avail themselves of the unhappy ascendancy which you have let them get over you. They make you commit faults and they incite you to an evil course without their seeming to have any part in it, in order to ruin you in my estimation.

"It is then to enlighten you that I send you my message; listen carefully to it, and pay attention to it, my children; it is the word of a father that loves you, and in whose eyes your interests are dear. I extinguish by these two belts of wampum the two fires which you lighted during the last two years, both at the Rock River and at White River. I extinguish them in such a way that not a single spark can escape."

A belt to the Demoiselle and to the Baril.

"My children: I have just told you that these are belts of wampum with which I extinguish the fires that you lighted, both at Rock River and at White River. By these belts I lift you from your mats and I lead you by the hand in order to bring you to Quiskakon, where I light your fire and make it more enduring than ever. It is in this country, my children, that you will enjoy a perfect peace, and where I will be ever at hand to give you marks of my friendship; it is in this country, my children, that you will enjoy the pleasures of life, it being the place where repose the bones of your ancestors, and those of M, de Vincennes,[66] whom you loved so much and who always governed you in such a way that your affairs were ever in good order. If you have forgotten the counsels which he gave you, these ashes shall recall to you the memory of them; the bones of your fathers suffer from your estrangement. Have pity on the dead who call you back to your village.

"Follow, along with your wives and your children, the chief whom I will send to bring you my message, and who will again light your fire at Quiskakon in such a manner that it shall no more be extinguished. I will afford you all the assistance which you have a right to expect from my friendship, and remember, my children, that I am doing for you what I have never done for any other nation."

Another speech with four belts of wampum for the Demoiselle, and two for the Baril:

"By these belts of wampum I set a boundary to all passages which lead to the Beautiful River, so that you go there no more, and that the English who are the ringleaders of every evil work may no longer approach this land, which belongs to me. I open for you at the same time an easy road to lead you to Kiskacon, where I will light your fire. I break off all trade with the English, whom I have notified to retire from off my territories; and if they come back there again they will have reason to be sorry for it."

Two belts of wampum to the Demoiselle, and two to the Baril.

"My children: When you shall have done what I have demanded of you, and which is only for your own advantage, I invite you to come to see me next year, and to receive from myself special marks of my friendship. I have extended the same invitation to all your brethren of the Beautiful River, and I hope that you will, one and all, have courage enough to respond to this invitation, as you ought; and in order to begin to give you a proof of my friendship, I send these presents to clothe your wives and your children. I add to them gunpowder and bullets, so that they may supply themselves more easily on the journey which you are going to make to Quiskacon. Abandon the land where you are; it is injurious to you, and avail yourselves of what I do for you."

The council over, every one retired. They carried away the presents to their village where they assembled to deliberate on their answer.
The 18th. About nine A. M., they came to give their answer.

Answers of the Demoiselle, chief of Miamis, established at the Rock River and of the Baril, established at White River, the 18th of September, 1749, with pipes of peace:

"It is an ancient custom among us when one speaks of agreeable affairs to present, first of all, pipes. We earnestly entreat you to listen to us. We are going to answer what you have asked of us. This pipe is a token of the pleasure which we have in smoking with you, and we hope to smoke the very same pipe with our father next year.

A belt.

"My father: Yesterday, we listened with pleasure to your speech. We have seen clearly that you are come only on a good mission. We have none other but good answers to give you. You have made us recall to memory the bones of forefathers, who mourn to see us in this place, and who remind us continually of it. You have made us a good road to return to our ancient home, and we thank you for it, my father, and we promise you to return thither immediately after the coming spring. We thank you for the kind words which you have addressed us. We see clearly that you have not forgotten us. Be convinced that we will labor to deal fairly with the Chauanones. We still remember the good advice which M. de Vincennes gave us. My father, you have to treat with people without spirit, and who are, perhaps, unable to answer well you as well as you hoped; but they will tell you the truth, for it is not from the lips that they speak to you, but from the bottom of their heart. You have bid us reflect seriously upon what you told us. We have done so, and we shall continue to do so during the whole winter. We hope to have the pleasure of making you a good speech this spring if the hunting is abundant. We will correct our faults, and we assure you, my father, that we will not listen to evil counsel, and that we will pay no attention to the rumors we hear at present."

Answer to the Demoiselle and the Baril in the same council, by M. de Celoron:

"I have listened to you my children, and I have weighed well your words. Whether you may not have understood me, or that you feign not to have done so, you do not answer to what I asked of you. I proposed to you on the part of your father Onontio, to come with me to Kiskakon to light there your fire and to build up your wigwam, but you put off doing so till next spring. I would have been delighted to be able to say to your father Onontio that I had brought you back. That would have caused him great pleasure on account of the interest he takes in all that concerns you. You give me your word that you will return there at the end of the winter. Be faithful then to your promise. You have assured him of this, because he is much stronger than you, and if you be wanting to it, fear the resentment of a father, who has only too much reason to be angry with you, and who has offered you the means of regaining his favor."

Answer to Celoron's speech by the Demoiselle and the Baril:

"My father, we shall be faithful in carrying out the promise that we have made you, and at the end of the winter we shall betake ourselves to our ancient habitation, and if the Master of Life favors our hunting, we hope to be able to repair our past faults; so be convinced that we do not speak from the end of our lips but from the bottom of the heart. We could not at present return whither you would have us go, for the season is too far advanced."

The council ended, I detained some of the old men for the purpose of finding out if what they had just said was sincere, so I spoke with these Indians who assured me that both the villages would return in the spring to Quiskakon, and all that kept them back was the fact of having no cabins built where I would conduct them, and that whilst hunting through the winter they were approaching their villages, and that they would return there absolutely. Rois, (the interpreter,) whom I had asked of M. de Raimond, arrived.

The 19th. I remained to endeavor by the agency of Rois, to induce the Demoiselle, along with some other chiefs, to come with me to light their fires and make their wigwams at Quiskakon, but I could not succeed in this. They kept always saying and assuring me that they would return thither next spring.

The 20th. All being ready for our setting out, we broke up our camp. After having burned our canoes, which were no longer of service for transportation, we set out on the march by land, each one carrying his provisions and baggage, except Messrs. the officers, for whom I had procured horses and some men to carry theirs. I had arranged all my men into four companies, each one of which had an officer at the right and another at the left. I led on the right and M. de Contrecoeur on the left.

We took only five days and a-half to accomplish this portage, which is thought to be fifty leagues.

The 25th. I arrived at M. de Raimond's, who commanded at Quiskakon. I stayed there only as long as was necessary to buy provisions and canoes to convey me to Detroit.

The 26th. I had called to me Cold Foot, chief of the Miamis established at Quiskakon, and others of note, to whom I repeated, in presence of M. de Raimond and the officers of my detachment, what I had said at the village of the Demoiselle and the answers I had got from them. After listening with much attention, he rose and said to me: "I hope I am deceived, but I am sufficiently attached to the interests of the French to say that the Demoiselle is a liar. It is the source of all my grief to be the only one who loves you, and to see all the nations of the south let loose against the French."

The 27th. I set out from M. de Raimond's, not having found a sufficient number of canoes for all my men, one part went by land under the conduct of some officers and the Indians who were to guide them through the woods. I took eight days to reach the lower part of the narrows,[67] where I arrived on the 6th of October, and found canoes and provisions for my detachment. I would have set out the same day if my Indians had followed me, but they amused themselves drinking in the lower Part of the River Miami.[68] I waited for them the 7th and 8th, and finally they arrived.

FATHER BONNECAMPS' REPORT

ACCOUNT OF THE VOYAGE ON THE BEAUTIFUL RIVER MADE IN 1749, UNDER THE DIRECTION OF MONSIEUR DE CELORON, BY FATHER BONNECAMPS.[69]

MONSIEUR,[70]

It was not possible for me last year, to give you an account of my voyage on the Beautiful River. All the vessels had left Quebec when I reached it. I could, it is true, have written you by way of New England; but I had many things to say to you which prudence would not allow me to send through the hands of the English. Therefore, in spite of the great desire that I had to respond to the confidence which you have shown me, I have chosen the alternative of deferring to do so, until the departure of our vessels.

We left la Chine on the 15th of June, toward 3 o'clock in the afternoon, numbering 23 canoes both French and savage. We slept at pointe Claire, about two leagues distant from la Chine. The next day, although starting out quite early, we made hardly more progress; and we gained les Cedres with much difficulty, because of the Cascades up which we had to ascend with our canoes, where the greater number were badly injured by the rocks.

The 17th. A part of the day was employed in mending them, and in doubling pointe des Cedres ("point of Cedars") with half-cargoes. At night, we camped on the shore of the lake; the place was a bare tongue of earth, very narrow, at the end of which was a considerable fall. The canoe of Monsieur de Joncaire unfortunately fell into the water there, and was lost; of the four men who were in it, three were fortunate enough to save themselves by swimming; the fourth was not so fortunate, and perished before our eyes, without our being able to give him the slightest aid. This was the only man whom we lost during the expedition.

The 18th. We reached ance aux bateaux ("boat cove"), which is at the entrance of lake St. Francis. On that day, Monsieur de Celoron detached a party of men to go to recover the remains of the wrecked canoe.

The 19th. I took our bearings at anse aux bateaux, which I found to be 45" 32' of latitude. The 21st. We passed lake St. Francis, which must be seven leagues in length, and two leagues in its greatest breadth. That night we slept at mille Roches ("thousand Rocks"). The 22nd. We arrived at the Long Sault toward eleven o'clock in the morning. There we made a portage of somewhat more than a quarter of a league, and reentered the canoes now empty of their lading. We would do much better to carry them by land, as we would carry baggage; we would lose less time, and incur less risk; but custom is a law against which good sense does not always prevail. The Long Sault is divided into three channels by two islands. The ascent is made by the north channel, and the descent by the south channel. The middle one, which is called "the lonely channel," is said to be impracticable.

The 25th. We disembarked at the dwelling of the abbe Piquet, whose new establishment is south of the river--37 leagues from Montreal, and directly at the end of the rapids. We found him lodged under a shelter of bark, in the midst of a clearing of nearly 40 arpents.[71] The fort which he has had constructed is a square of 70 feet on each side; it is situated at the mouth of a river, which he has named la Presentation, and at the base of a little headland, low and marshy. According to abbe Piquet, the soil is excellent; but it did not appear so to us. One sees there as many trees of fir as of hard wood. His whole village consisted of two men, who followed us into the Beautiful River.

The 27th. We arrived at Cataracoui, soon after noon. The fort of Cataracoui[72] is situated near the bottom of a cove, about thirty arpents from the river. It is a square of stone-work, 60 toises[73] in extent, each corner being flanked by a bastion.[74] Opposite the entrance, a small demilune[75] has been constructed. The neighborhood of the fort is very open, and liable to surprise. It is slightly commanded by a little hill, not very far away. The 28th. I observed its latitude, which I found to be 44" 28'. It is here that the course of the river St. Lawrence properly begins, which, in my judgment, does not exceed 230 leagues. The 29th. A strong wind from the southwest detained us at Cataracoui.

The 30th. The lake being calm, we took the route to Niagara, where we arrived on the 6th of July. In all the passage of lake Ontario, I have seen nothing which could excite curiosity. I will only tell you that the waters of this lake are very clear and transparent; at 17 and 18 feet, the bottom can be seen as distinctly as if one saw it through a polished glass. They have still another property, very pleasant to travelers,--that of retaining great coolness in the midst of the suffocating heat which one is sometimes obliged to endure in passing this lake.

The Fort of Niagara is a square made of palisades, faced on the outside with oak timbers, which bind and strengthen the whole work. A large stone barrack[76] forms the curtain-wall, which overlooks the lake; its size is almost the same as that of Fort Frontenac. It is situated on the eastern bank of the channel[77] by which the waters of lake Erie discharge themselves. It will soon be necessary to remove it elsewhere, because the bank, being continually undermined by the waves which break against it, is gradually caving in, and the water gains noticeably on the fort. It would be advantageously placed above the waterfall, on a fine plateau where all canoes are obliged to land to make the portage. Thus the savages, people who are naturally lazy, would be spared the trouble of making three leagues by land; and if the excessive price of merchandise could be diminished, that would insensibly disgust the English, and we could see the trade, which is almost entirely ruined, again flourishing.

On the 6th and the 7th, I observed the western amplitude of the sun, when it set in the lake; that gave me 6" 30' Northwest for the variation of compass. The latitude of the fort is 43" 28'.

On the 8th, the entire detachment arrived at the portage. The 12th. We encamped at the little rapid at the entrance of lake Erie. The channel which furnishes communication between the two lakes is about 9 leagues in length. Two leagues above the fort, the portage begins. There are three hills to climb, almost in succession. The 3rd is extraordinarily high and steep; it is, at its summit, at least 300 feet above the level of the water. If I had had my graphometer, I could have ascertained its exact height; but I had left that instrument at the fort, for fear that some accident might happen to it during the rest of the voyage. When the top of this last hill is reached, there is a level road to the other end of the portage; the road is broad, fine, and smooth. The famous waterfall of Niagara is very nearly equidistant from the two lakes. It is formed by a rock cleft vertically, and is 133 feet, according to my measurement, which I believe to be exact. Its figure is a half-ellipse, divided near the middle by a little island. The width of the fall is perhaps three-eighths of a league. The water falls in foam over the length of the rock, and is received in a large basin, over which hangs a continual mist.

The 13th. We remained in our camp at the little rapid to await our savages, who were amusing themselves with drinking rum at the portage, with a band of their comrades who were returning from Choaguen (Oswego).[78] The 14th. The savages having rejoined us, we entered lake Erie, but a strong southwest wind having arisen, we put back to shore. The 15th. In the morning, the wind having ceased, we continued our route and on the 16th, we arrived early at the portage of Yjadakoin.

It began at the mouth of a little stream called Riviere aux pommes ("apple River"),--the 3rd that is met after entering the lake, and thus it may be easily recognized. The 15th. In the evening, I observed the variation, which I found to be nothing.

We always kept close to the shore. It is quite regular, straight, but moderately high, and furnishes little shelter; in many places it is mere rock, covered with a few inches of soil. Lake Erie is not deep; its waters have neither the transparency nor the coolness of those of lake Ontario. It is at this lake that I saw for the first time the wild turkeys; they differ in no way from our domestic turkeys.

The 17th. We began the portage, and made a good league that day. I observed the latitude at the 2nd station, -- that is, half a league from the lake, -- and I found it 42° 33'. The 18th. Our people being fatigued, we shortened the intervals between the stations, and we hardly made more than half a league. 19th. Bad weather did not allow us to advance far; nevertheless we gained ground every day, and, the 22nd, the portage was entirely accomplished.

In my judgment, it is three and a half leagues. The road is passably good. The wood through which it is cut resembles our forests in France. The beech, the ash, the elm, the red and white oak--these trees compose the greater part of it. A species of tree is found there, which has no other name than that of "the unknown tree." Its trunk is high, erect, and almost without , branches to the top. It has a light, soft wood, which is used for making pirogues, and is good for that alone. Eyes more trained than ours, would, perhaps, have made discoveries which would have pleased the taste of arborists. Having reached the shore of lake Yjadakoin, Monsieur de Celoron thought it well to pass the rest of the day in camp to give his people a breathing-space. On the morning of the 23rd, we examined the provisions, pitched the canoes, and set out. Before starting, I took advantage of the fine weather to get the latitude, which I found to be 42" 30'. Lake Yjadakoin may be a league and a half in its greatest width, and

6 leagues in its entire length. It becomes narrow near the middle, and seems to form a double lake.

We left it on the morning of the 24th, and entered the little river which bears its name, and which is, as it were, its outlet. After a league and a half of still water, one enters a rapid, which extends for three leagues or more; in times of drouth, it is very shallow. We were told that in the spring, or after heavy rains, it is navigable; as for us, we found it drained dry. In certain places, which were only too frequent, there was barely two or three inches of water.

Before entering this place, Monsieur de Celoron had the greater part of the baggage unloaded, with people to carry it to the rendezvous. On the road, our natives noticed fresh trails, and huts newly abandoned. From these unequivocal indications, we inferred that some one had come to spy upon us, and that at our approach our discoverers had carried the alarm to the Beautiful River. Therefore, Monsieur the Commandant held a council on the morning of the 25th, in which, after having declared your intentions, he proposed to send Monsieur de Joncaire to la paille coupee, to carry thither some porcelain branches,[79] and to invite the natives to listen to the peaceful message of their father Onontio. The proposition was unanimously approved, and Monsieur de Joncaire set out, accompanied by a detachment of savages. We then worked at repairing our canoes, and sent them on, half-loaded. On the morning of the 27th, we again found the still water, on which we advanced tranquilly until half past 10 on the 28th, --a fatal hour, which plunged us again into our former miseries. The water suddenly gave out under our canoes, and we were reduced to the sad necessity of dragging them over the stones, -- whose sharp edges, in spite of our care and precautions, took off large splinters from time to time. Finally, overcome with weariness, and almost despairing of seeing the Beautiful River, we entered it on the 29th, at noon. Monsieur de Celoron buried a plate of lead on the south bank of the Ohio; and, farther down, he attached the royal coat of arms to a tree. After these operations, we encamped opposite a little Iroquois village, of 12 or 13 cabins; it is called Kananouangon.

The 30th. We arrived at la paille coupee. There we rejoined Monsieur de Joncaire, who told us that our conjecture was correct; that the report of our march had thrown all those people into consternation, and that he had had much difficulty in making the fugitives return. The chiefs came to greet Monsieur the Commandant, who bestowed upon them a thousand tokens of kindness, and sought to reassure them.

The 31st. In the morning, he spoke to them on your behalf; and in the evening he received their reply, that every one had been satisfied,--if one could believe it sincere; but we did not doubt that it was extorted by fear.

You will excuse me from reporting here, or elsewhere, either the words of Monsieur de Celoron, or the replies which they gave him, because he will send you copies of these.

La paille coupee is a very insignificant village, composed of Iroquois and some Loups. It is situated on the northern bank of the Ohio, and is bounded on the north by a group of mountains which form a very narrow half-basin, at the bottom of which is the village; its latitude is 42" 5'.

On the 1st of August we broke camp; and that evening we slept at a little Loup village of 9 or 10 cabins. We marched all day between two chains of mountains, which border the river on the right and left. The Ohio is very low during the first twenty leagues; but a great storm, which we had experienced on the eve of our departure, had swollen the waters, and we pursued our journey without any hindrance.

Monsieur Chabert[80] on that day caught seven rattlesnakes, which were the first that I had seen This snake differs in no way from others, except that its tail is terminated by seven or eight little scales, fitting one into another, which make a sort of clicking sound when the creature moves or shakes itself. Some have yellowish spots scattered over a brown ground, and others are entirely brown, or almost black.

There are, I am told, very large ones. None of those which I have seen exceed 4 feet. The bite is fatal. It is said that washing the wound which has been received, with saliva mixed with a little sea-salt, is a sovereign remedy. We have not had, thank God, any occasion to put this antidote to the test. I have been told a thousand marvelous things about this reptile; among others, that the squirrel, upon perceiving a rattlesnake, immediately becomes greatly agitated; and, at the end of a certain period of time, -- drawn, as it were, by an invincible attraction, -- approaches it, even throwing itself into the jaws of the serpent. I have read a statement similar to this reported in philosophic transactions; but I do not give it credence, for all that.

The 2nd. Monsieur de Celoron spoke to the Loups. I took the bearing of our camp on the same day, and found it to be 41" 41' of latitude.

The 3rd. We continued our route, and we marched, as on the first day, buried in the somber and dismal valley, which serves as the bed of the

Ohio. We encountered on route two small villages of Loups, where we did not halt. In the evening, after we disembarked, we buried a 2nd plate of lead under a great rock, upon which were to be seen several figures roughly graven. These were the figures of men and women, and the footprints of goats, turkeys, bears, etc., traced upon the rock. Our officers tried to persuade me that this was the work of Europeans; but, in truth, I may say that in the style and workmanship of these engravings one cannot fail to recognize the unskillfulness of savages. I might add to this, that they have much analogy with the hieroglyphics which they use instead of writing.

The 4th. We continued our route, always surrounded by mountains, -- sometimes so high that they did not permit us to see the sun before 9 or 10 o'clock in the morning, or after 2 or 3 in the afternoon. This double chain of mountains stretches along the Beautiful River, at least as far as riviere a la Poche ("Rocky river"). Here and there, they fall back from the shore, and display little plains of one or two leagues in depth.

The 6th. We arrived at Atigue, where we found no person; all the people had fled to the woods. Seeing this, we went on, and came to the old village of the Chaouanons, where we found only a man and a woman, so old that their united ages would make fully two centuries. Some time afterward, we encountered five Englishmen who appeared to us to be engages; they were ordered to quit that region, and they responded that they were ready to obey. They were given a letter for the governor of Philadelphia; it was a copy of that which you had given for a model. These English came from Chiningue and Sinhioto. They had some forty packets of peltries, which they were preparing to carry to Philadelphia. These packets consisted of skins of bears, otters, cats, precans, and roe-deer, with the hair retained,--for neither martens nor beavers are seen there. The Englishmen told us that they reckoned it 100 leagues from that place to Philadelphia.

The 7th. We found another village of Loups. Monsieur de Celoron induced the chief to come to Chiningue to hear your message. At two leagues from there we landed, in order to speak to the English; the same compliments were presented to them as to the others, and they answered us with the same apparent submission. They were lodged in miserable cabins, and had a storehouse well filled with peltries, which we did not disturb.

One of our officers showed me a bean-tree. This is a tree of medium

71

size whose trunk and branches are armed with thorns three or four inches long, and two or three lines thick at the base. The interior of these thorns is filled with pulp. The fruit is a sort of little bean, enclosed in a pod about a foot long, an inch wide, and of a reddish color somewhat mingled with green. There are five or six beans in each pod. The same day, we dined in a hollow cottonwood tree, in which 29 men could be ranged side by side. This tree is not rare in those regions; it grows on the river-banks and in marshy places. It attains a great height and has many branches. Its bark is seamed and rough like shagreen. The wood is hard, brittle, and apt to decay; I do not believe that I have seen two of these trees that were not hollow. Its leaves are large and thickly set; its fruit is of the size of a hazelnut, enveloped in down; the whole resembling an apple, exactly spherical, and about an inch in diameter.

Now that I am on the subject of trees, I will tell you something of the assimine-tree, and of that which is called the lentil-tree. The first is a shrub, the fruit of which is oval in shape, and a little larger than a bustard's egg; its substance is white and spongy, and becomes yellow when the fruit is ripe. It contains two or three kernels, large and flat like the garden bean. They have each their special cell. The fruits grow ordinarily in pairs, and are suspended on the same stalk. The French have given it a name which is not very refined, Testiculi asini. This is a delicate morsel for the savages and the Canadians; as for me, I have found it of an unendurable insipidity. The one which I call the lentil-tree is a tree of ordinary size; the leaf is short, oblong, and serrated all around. Its fruit much resembles our lentils. It is enclosed in pods, which grow in large, thick tufts at the extremities of the branches. But it is time to resume our course.

On the morning of the 8th, Monsieur de Celoron sent me with an officer to examine certain writings, which our savages had seen the evening before, on a rock, and which they imagined to contain some mystery. Having examined it, we reported to him that this was nothing more than three or four English names scrawled with charcoal. I took the altitude in our camp, the latitude of which was 40" 46'.

A little after noon, we departed for the village of the Chiningue. It was three o'clock when we arrived. We disembarked at the foot of a very high slope. It was lined with people, and they saluted us with four volleys from their guns; we responded in the same manner.

Monsieur de Celoron, reflecting upon the disadvantageous situation of his camp, if we remained at the foot of the slope, decided to have it transported to the top, and to place our force between the village and the woods. This move was executed in sight of the savages, who dared not oppose us. When we were well established, the chiefs came to salute the Commandant. After an interchange of compliments, Monsieur de Celoron manifested his displeasure that they had set up the English flag opposite that of France, and ordered them to take it down. The firm tone with which he spoke caused them to obey him. In the evening we doubled the guard; and, instead of 40 men who had mounted guard regularly every night since our entrance into Yjadakoin, 80 were assigned to that duty. Moreover, all the officers and engages were ordered to sleep in their clothing.

On the morning of the 9th, a savage came to tell Monsieur de Joncaire that 80 warriors starting from Kaskaske[81] were on the point of arriving; that they came intending to aid their brothers, and to deal us a blow.

Monsieur de Joncaire, having made his report of this to the Commandant, the latter immediately gave orders to prepare for a warm reception of the enemy. These preparations were not made. The savages, seeing our bold front and our superior number, quietly withdrew and saluted us very politely in passing before our camp. During the rest of the day, all was tranquil.

On the 10th, there was a council, in which Monsieur de Celoron spoke to them on your part. They responded on the 11th, and we departed immediately after the council. The village of Chiningue is quite new; it is hardly more than five or six years since it was established. The savages who live there are almost all Iroquois; they count about sixty warriors. The English there were 10 in number, and one among them was their chief. Monsieur de Celoron had him come, and ordered him, as he had done with the others, to return to his own country. The Englishman, who saw us ready to depart, acquiesced in all that was exacted from him,--firmly resolved, doubtless, to do nothing of the kind, as soon as our backs were turned.

From Chiningue to Sinhioto, my journal furnishes me with nothing curious or new; there are only readings of the compass, taken every quarter of an hour, the list of which would be as tedious for the reader as for the copyist. I will only tell you that we buried three plates of lead at the mouths of three different rivers, the 1st of which was called Kanonouaora, the second Jenanguekona, and the 3rd, Chinodaichta. It was in the neighborhood of this river that we began to see the Illinois cattle;[82] but, here and elsewhere, they were in such small numbers that our men could hardly kill a score of them. It was, besides, necessary to seek them far in the woods. We had been assured, however, at our departure, that at each point we should find them by hundreds, and that the tongues alone of those which we should kill would suffice to support the troops. This is not the first time when I have experienced that hyperbole and exaggeration were figures familiar to the Canadians.

When we were near Sinhioto, Monsieur de Celoron, by the advice of the officers and of the savages, despatched Messieurs de Joncaire and Niverville to announce our approaching arrival to the Chaouanons. Their reception was not gracious. Hardly had the savages perceived them, when they fired on them, and their colors were pierced in three places. In spite of this hail of musketry, they advanced as far as the bank, and disembarked without receiving any wound. They were conducted to the council-cabin; but scarcely had Monsieur de Joncaire commenced his harangue, when a miserable Panis (Pawnee), to all appearances influenced by the English, suddenly arose, crying out that they were deceived, and that the French came to them only to destroy them. This denunciation was like a war-cry. The savages ran to arms, and arrested our envoys; they talked of binding them to the stake; and perhaps they would have executed this threat if an Iroquois, who was by chance present, had not appeased the furious savages by assuring them that we had no evil designs. He even promised to go with Monsieur de Joncaire to meet us, which he did.

We encountered them on the 22nd, about a league from the village. Monsieur de Celoron thanked the Iroquois for the zeal which he had displayed on this occasion, and made him some small presents.

We finally embarked, in order to go to Sinhioto. We encamped opposite the village, where we worked hard, in order to complete the fort, which had been begun the evening before.

On the 23rd, a council was held; but the savages raised some difficulties about the place where they were to assemble. They desired that we should address them in the cabin appointed for Councils; Monsieur de Celoron declared, on the contrary, that it was for the children to come to hear the words of their father in the place where he had lighted his fire. Briefly, after many disputes, the savages gave way and presented themselves in our camp. During the Council, two couriers arrived, to announce that canoes bearing the French colors had been seen descending the river of Sinhioto. This news somewhat disconcerted our grave senators, who imagined that it was a party of warriors sent against them from Detroit, and that it was our design to inclose them between two fires. Monsieur the Commandant had great difficulty to reassure them. Finally, however, their fears were dissipated, and they continued the Council. The 24th. The savages responded, but in vague and general terms, which signified nothing at all.

On the 25th, four Outaouas[83] arrived with letters from Monsieur (de) Sabrevois, which notified Monsieur de Celoron that he had not been able to persuade the savages of his government to come to join us on the Beautiful River, as had been projected. In the evening, there was a bonfire to celebrate the feast of St. Louis. All the detachment was under arms; they fired three volleys of musketry, preceded by several cries of Vive le Roy!

The 26th. The Chaouanons gave a 2nd response which was somewhat more satisfactory than the 1st. After which, we continued our journey to riviere a la Roche. The situation of the village of the Chaouanons is quite pleasant, -- at least, it is not masked by the mountains, like the other villages through which we had passed. The Sinhioto river, which bounds it an the West, has given it its name. It is composed of about sixty cabins. The English men there numbered five. They were ordered to withdraw, and promised to do so. The latitude of our camp was 39" 1'

The 28th. We encamped at the mouth of riviere Blanche ("White river"), where we found a small band of Miamis with their chief, named le Baril ("the Barrel"). They had established themselves there a short time before, and formed a village of 7 or 8 cabins, a league distant from the river. Monsieur de Celoron requested them to accompany him to the village of la Demoiselle ("the young Lady"), and they promised to do so. We passed two days waiting for them. Finally, on the morning of the 31st, they appeared, followed by their women, their children, and their dogs. All embarked, and about 4 o'clock in the afternoon we entered riviere a la Roche, after having buried the 6th and last leaden plate on the western bank of that river, and to the north of the Ohio.

This Beautiful River -- so little known to the French, and, unfortunately, too well known to the English -- is according to my estimate, 181 marine leagues from the mouth of the Yjadakoin (or Tjadakoin) to the entrance of riviere a la Roche. In all this distance, we have counted twelve villages established on its banks; but if one penetrate into the small continent enclosed between lake Erie and the Ohio, one will find it, according to what has been told us, much more populous. We have been specially told of a certain village situated on the river Kaskaske, in which, we are assured, there are nearly 800 men. Each village, whether large or small, has one or more traders, who have in their employ engages for the transportation of peltries. Behold, then, the English already far within our territory; and, what is worse, they are under the protection of a crowd of savages whom they entice to themselves, and whose number increases every day. Their design is, without doubt, to establish themselves there; and, if efficacious measures be not taken as soon as possible to arrest their progress, we run very great risk of seeing ourselves quickly driven from the upper countries, and of being obliged to confine ourselves to the limits which it may please those gentlemen to prescribe to us. This is perhaps all the more true that it does not seem probable. I resume the thread of my journal.

Riviere a la Roche is very well named. Its bottom is but one continuous rock; its waters are extremely shallow. Notwithstanding this, we had the good fortune to guide our canoes as far as the village of la Demoiselle. In order to lighten them, we had landed half of our people. This was thought to have (occasioned) the loss of Monsieur de Joannes,[84]--who, having undertaken to follow a savage who was going to hunt, lost himself in the woods, and remained there two days without our being able to obtain any news of him, in spite of all the efforts which we made. On the 3rd day after his disappearance, we saw him, when we least expected to do so, at a bend in the river, conducted by two Miamis.

On the 13th of September, we had the honor of saluting la Demoiselle in his fort. It is situated on a vast prairie which borders Riviere a la Roche; its latitude is 40" 34'. This band is not numerous; it consists at most of 40 or 50 men. There is among them an English trader. Monsieur de Celoron did not talk with la Demoiselle until the 17th, because he awaited an interpreter from the Miamis, for whom he had asked Monsieur Raimond. But, wearied with waiting, and seeing the season already advanced, he determined to take for an interpreter an old Sounantouan who was in le Baril's company.

On the 18th, la Demoiselle replied, and in his answer promised to take back his band to their old village in the following spring; he even gave his word that he would go with us as far as there, in order to prepare everything for his return. But the arrival of the Miami interpreter put him in a bad humor; he forgot all his promises, and in spite of all that we could do, he constantly refused to see us. We then left him; and, after having burned our canoes and all that we could not carry, we took leave of him on the morning of the 20th.

Our journey by land was only five days. We were divided into four brigades, each commanded by two officers. We marched in single file, because the narrowness of the path would not permit us to do otherwise. The road was passable, but we found it quite tedious. In my estimation, the journey from la Demoiselle's to the Miamis might cover 35 leagues. Three times we crossed Riviere a la Roche; but here it was only a feeble brook, which ran over a few feet of mud. A little more than half-way, we began to skirt the river of the Miamis, which was on our left. We found therein large crabs in abundance. From time to time we marched over vast prairies, where the herbage was sometimes of extraordinary height. Having reached Monsieur Raimond's post, we bought pirogues and provisions; and, on the afternoon of the 27th, We set out, en route for Detroit.

The fort of the Miamis was in a very bad condition when we reached it; most of the palisades were decayed and fallen into ruin. Within there were eight houses, -- or, to speak more correctly, eight miserable huts, which only the desire of making money could render endurable. The French there numbered 22; all of them, even to the commandant, had the fever. Monsieur Raimond did not approve the situation of the fort, and maintained that it should be placed on the bank of the St. Joseph river, distant only a scant league from its present site. He wished to show me that spot, but the hindrances of our departure prevented me from going thither. All that I could do for him was to trace for him the plan of his new fort. The latitude of the old one is 41" 29'. It was while with the Miamis that I learned that we had, a little before entering riviere a la Roche, passed within two or three leagues of the famous salt-springs where are the skeletons of immense animals. This news greatly chagrined me; and I could hardly forgive myself for having missed this discovery. It was the more curious that I should have done this on my journey, and I would have been proud if I could have given you the details of it.

The Miami River caused us no less embarrassment than Riviere a la Roche had done. At almost every instant we were stopped by beds of flat stones, over which it was necessary to drag our pirogues by main force.

I will say, however, that at intervals were found beautiful reaches of smooth water, but they were few and short. In the last six leagues, the river is broad (and deep), and seems to herald the grandeur of the lake into which it discharges its waters. At 6 leagues above lake Erie, I took the altitude, which was found to be 42" 0'.

We entered the lake on the 5th of October. On entering it, there is to the left the bay of Onanguisse, which is said to be very deep. Soon after, one encounters to the right, the Isles aux Serpents ("islands where there are Snakes"). On the 6th, we arrived at the mouth of the Detroit River, where we found canoes and provisions for our return. Monsieur de Celoron had the goodness to permit me to go to the fort[85] with some officers. We spent there the entire day of the 7th. I took the latitude in Father Bonaventure's courtyard, and I found it 42" 38'·

In the evening, we returned to our camp, where we spent the 8th waiting for our savages, a class of men created in order to exercise the patience of those who have the misfortune to travel with them. I profited by this hindrance in order to take the latitude of our camp, which was 42" 28'.

I remained too short a time at Detroit to be able to give you an exact description of it. All that I can say to you about it is, that its situation appeared to me charming. A beautiful river runs at the foot of the fort; vast plains, which only ask to be cultivated, extend beyond the sight. There is nothing milder than the climate, which scarcely counts two months of winter. The productions of Europe, and especially the grains, grow much better than in many of the cantons of France. It is the Touraine and Beauce of Canada. Moreover, we should regard Detroit[86] as one of the most important posts of the Colony. It is conveniently situated for furnishing aid to Michilimakinak, to the St. Joseph River,[87] to the Bay,[88] to the Miamis, Ouiatanons,[89] and to the Beautiful River, supposing that settlements be made thereon. Accordingly, we cannot send thither too many people; but where shall we find men therefor? Certainly not in Canada. The colonists whom you sent there last year contented themselves with eating the rations that the King provided. Some among them, even, carried away by their natural levity, have left the country and gone to seek their fortune elsewhere. How many poor laborers in France would be delighted to find a country which could furnish them abundantly with what would repay them for their industry and toil.

The Fort of Detroit is a long square; I do not know its dimensions,[90] but it appeared large to me. The village of the Hurons and that of the Outaouas are on the other side of the river,--(where father La Richardie told me, the rebels were beginning to disperse, and the band of Nicolas was diminishing day by day. We had asked news about him, when upon the Beautiful river;) and were told he had established his residence in the neighborhood of lake Erie.

We left Detroit on the 9th of October, and on the 19th arrived at Niagara. I took the altitude twice on lake Erie,-- once at Pointe Pelee,[91] which was 42" 20'; the other time, a little below pointe a la Biche ("Fawn's point"), which was 43" 6': We left Niagara on the 22nd, and, to shorten our road, we passed along the south shore of lake Ontario. We experienced on this lake some terrible storms. More than once, we were on the point of perishing. Finally, notwithstanding the winds and tempests, our bark canoes brought us safe and sound to Cataracoui on the 4th of November. I saw Choaguen in passing, but it was too far for me to examine it.

On the 7th, we left Cataracoui, and on the 10th we arrived at Montreal. On the road we halted at the dwelling of abbe Piquet, who was then at Montreal. We found three-quarters of his fort burned by the Iroquois--sent, they say, for this purpose, by the English. At one of the angles of the fort they had caused to be constructed a little redout after the style of the Fort St. Jean.[92] The fire had spared it. In returning: I shot all the rapids, the danger of which had been rather exaggerated to me. The first that one encounters in going out from abbe Piquet's is les Galaux ("the Gallops"); it is a very small matter. The rapide Plat ("Flat rapid") which succeeds it is of still less importance. The Long Sault has its difficulties. It is necessary to have a quick eye and sure hand, in order to avoid on the one side the Cascade, and on the other a great rock -- against which a canoe, were it of bronze, would be shattered like glass. The Coteau du Lac is not difficult, because one passes at a considerable distance from the Cascade. In the passage of les Cedres, there is no risk except for bark canoes, because the water has but little depth. "The Thicket" and "the Hole" are two difficult places; but, after all, one escapes save for shipping a little water while shooting this rapid. I have not shot "the Hole." Our guide led us by another way, which was not much better. It was necessary to cross a very violent current, which will precipitate you into a very deep cascade, if you miss the right point for crossing. One of our canoes came near turning a somersault, not having taken proper precautions. The Sault St. Louis is perfectly well known to you.

On the 14th. Monsieur de Celoron and I set out for Quebec, where we arrived on the 18th of November,--that is to say, five months and eighteen days after having left it.

I beg of you a few moments' further audience, in behalf of the chart which I have the honor to present to you. It is reduced, on account of its great extent; it has 20 fixed points which have been furnished to me by the latitudes observed, and which I have marked with double crosses. The longitude is everywhere estimated. If I had had a good compass, I would have been able to determine several of its points by observation; but could I or ought I to rely on a compass of indifferent merit, and of which I have a hundred times proved the irregularity, both before and since my return? Can I dare say that my estimates are correct? In truth, this would be very rash, -- especially as we were obliged to navigate currents subject to a thousand alternations. In still water, even, what rules of estimation could one have, of which the correctness would not be disturbed by the variation and inequalities of the wind or of the rowers? As for the points of the compass, I can answer for having observed them all, and marked them in my journal with the utmost care; because I know that a part of the exactness of my chart depends upon it. I have not failed to correct them according to the variations that I have observed. I have similarly corrected the leagues of distance, when such did not accord with the latitude observed. In a word. I have done my utmost to deserve the marks of esteem which you have had the goodness to bestow upon me. If I have been fortunate enough to succeed, I beg of you to deign to employ me, when occasion therefor shall present itself; that is the only recompense which I expect for my work.

I cannot bring myself to finish this letter without rendering to Messieurs our officers all the justice that they merit. In the subalterns I have admired their zeal for the service, their courage when occasion required it, their submission to the orders of the Commandant, and their promptitude in exercising them.

As for Monsieur de Celoron, he is a man attentive, clearsighted, and active; firm, but pliant when necessary; fertile in resources, and full of resolution, --a man, in fine, made to command. I am no flatterer, and I do not fear that what I have said should make me pass for one.

I have the honor to be with the most profound respect,
MONSIEUR,
Your very humble and very obedient servant,
At Quebec, October 17, 1750

DE BONNECAMPS, S. J.

NOTES

1. Pierre-Joseph Céloron de Blainville was born in Montreal, December 29, 1693. He entered colonial military service in 1707, as a cadet and was commissioned in 1712. In 1739, he reached the rank of captain. Céloron commanded many western posts in New France including Michilimackinac, Detroit, and Niagara and led the western detachment to the Chickasaw War of 1739. Needing an able commander, he was given command of Fort St. Frederic during King George's War (1747). After the war and the Ohio expedition, he had difficulty in relationships with others in Detroit and was given the position of Town-Major at Montreal. Céloron died April 12, 1759. (See the **Dictionary of Canadian Biography, III.**)

2. The Order of Saint Louis was an award sought by all Canadian officers. Besides the prestige, it carried a pension.

3. La Belle Riviere, the Beautiful River, was the French name for the Ohio River and the Allegheny River, which they saw as one continuous body of water.

4. Roland-Michel Barrin de La Galissonière, Marquis de La Galissonière, was born at Rochefort in 1693. He entered the navy in 1710, becoming a Captain and Knight of the Order of St. Louis in 1738. He arrived in New France in 1747, sent to replace the Marquis de La Jonquière who had been unable to assume the post. He returned to France in 1749. (See the **Dictionary of Canadian Biography, III.**)

5. La Chine was a short distance up river from Montreal and the traditional starting point for western expeditions.

6. Cadets were usually boys or young men who were training to be officers. They ranked as elder soldiers and were directly responsible to the sergeants. Despite their time of service, they had to wait until there was a vacancy in the ranks of officers to obtain a commission. As there were few other options for earning a living in New France, officers

tended not to retire. Consequently, without a war that created openings through death or expansion of the service, cadets might have a long wait to become an ensign.

7. Father Bonnecamps, S.J. (See note 69.)

8. These Iroquois were related to the confederacy located in central New York allied to the British. They had settlements near Montreal and were allied to the French through the missionaries that had induced them to settle in this area.

9. An alliance of tribes in present-day Maine and the Canadian Maritimes. Some relocated to Catholic missions in central Canada.

10. Pointe Claire was a few miles from La Chine on the north side of *Lac St. Louis*. It was customary to travel only a short distance the first day so that any equipment problems or shortages could be accommodated before the party had gone further into the wilderness.

11. Coteau de Cedres is at the western end of *Lac St. Louis*.

12. Probably Philippe Chabert de Joncaire. See note 29.

13. Francis Piquet, 1708-1781. This mission-fort, La Presentation, was at present-day Ogdensburg, New York. The site was abandoned in 1759, by the French to the oncoming English Army under General Jeffery Amherst.

14. Tribe that inhabited an area adjacent to the St. Lawrence River east of Quebec.

15. Fort Frontenac had first been established in 1683 at the junction of the St. Lawrence River and Lake Ontario (Kingston, Ontario), and then abandoned. It was reestablished in 1695.

16. Also known as Kente. It was on the north shore of Lake Ontario, probably near Trenton, Ontario.

17. Charles Francois Xavier Tarieu de La Naudiere et de La Perade, (dit La Perade-Chaudiere). 1710-1776. La Naudiere was commission in 1724, and fought against Fox/Sauk in 1736. He became a captain in 1751. He served with Montcalm's Army in the final French and Indian War and was awarded the Order of St. Louis.

18. Probably refers to Fort Miamis a military and trading post at present-day Fort Wayne, Indiana.

19. Many tribes established villages near the French settlement at Detroit, including Ottawas, Hurons, and Wyandots.

20. Charles Jacques de Sabrevois de Bleury, 1699?-1774. Sabrevois was acting commandant Detroit 1734-1738, and served in the Chickasaw campaign 1739. As Celoron says, he returned to Detroit, 1749-1751.

21. Fort Niagara was built in 1726-1727, on Lake Ontario at the mouth of the Niagara River.

22. Paul Joseph Le Moyne de Longueuil, Chevalier de Longueuil 1701-1778, was born near Montreal. He was promoted to Captain in 1727, and was commander at Detroit 1743-1749, 1752. Longueuil received the Order of St. Louis in 1744. His final post was Governor of Three Rivers, 1757-1760.

23. Claude Pierre Pecaudy de Contrecoeur, 1705/1706-1776, was born in New France. His long career in the west included building Fort Duquesne (Pittsburgh, Pennsylvania) and being in command on the Ohio during Braddock's defeat in 1755. He was awarded the Order of St. Louis in 1756.

24. The translation used the word, squadrons. Piquets has been substituted as the term commonly used and probably used in the original. This is best translated as, detachments.

25. This was the portage from Lake Erie to Chautauqua Lake. This route was used until the establishment of Fort Presque Isle (Erie, Pennsylvania) in 1753.

26. Louis Coulon de Villiers, 1710-1757, was born at Vercheres (Quebec) and became one of the best known officers in New France. He served many years in the west and commanded the troops that defeated George Washington at Fort Necessity in 1754. After service in the Oswego Campaign in 1756, and Fort William Henry in 1757, he received the Order of St. Louis. He died of smallpox in 1757.

27. Paul Le Borques (Le Borgne), 1717?-1789? He and his two sons were with Celoron.

28. At the junction of the Allegheny River and Conewango Creek.

29. At the junction of the Allegheny River and Broken Straw Creek.

30. Original translation has, Barques. Assuming this is a "typo," it has been changed.

31. There were various "league" measurements in use in the eighteenth century. The common league was 2.76 English miles.

32. Philippe Thomas Dagneau Douville de La Saussaye, 1727-1757, was commissioned in 1755, and (possibly) killed near Fort Duquesne in 1757.

33. Term used by the Indians for the Governor-General of Canada.

34. The Chabert de Joncaire family was long associated with Indian affairs in western New York and Pennsylvania. French-born Louis Thomas, had been a captive of the Senecas and adopted into the nation. His sons', Philippe Thomas (the lieutenant mentioned here), 1707-1766, and Daniel, 1714-1771, had been instructed in Indian affairs, undoubtedly the reason they were with Celoron. Philippe-Thomas was awarded the Order of St. Louis and went to France after the war. Daniel remained in Canada and died in Detroit.

35. Brandy

36. Senecas

37. The Iroquois confederacy of the Mohawks, Oneidas, Onondagas, Cayugas, and Senecas.

38. French name for the Delaware.

39. French for the Fox (Mesquakie). This nation had fought the French for half a century in northern Wisconsin. The French conducted a devastating campaign in the early 1730's to totally destroy the Mesquakie nation, in which they nearly succeeded. The number of Renards in this village was probably small. (See Edmunds and Peyser, **The Fox Wars**. Norman: University of Oklahoma Press 1993.)

40. This is French Creek at present-day Franklin, Pennsylvania. When the French established forts in western Pennsylvania (1753-1754), they built Fort Machault using the cabins of John Fraser, an English trader. After the English conquest, Fort Venango was established. It was captured by the Indians in the uprising of 1763 (Pontiac's Rebellion).

41. This village name causes some confusion. There may have been more than one Attigua in existence during this period. A 1755 map shows a village of this name on the Riviere aux Boeufs (French Creek) and a Loup village of this name further down the Ohio. Céloron was probably referring to the latter.

42. Former Shawnee village at the junction of Bull Creek and the Allegheny River.

43. Charles de Beauharnois de la Boische, 1671-1749. Governor-General of New France 1726-1747.

44. The War of the Austrian Succession called King George's War in North America, 1744-1748.

45. The French flag at this time was white, therefore, this should not be seen as a parley or surrender signal.

46. Aliquippa.

47. This and Chavenois are Shawnee.

48. Probably the trading center the English called Logstown, present-day Beaver, Pennsylvania.

49. Nippissing.

50. Ottawas.

51. Probably refers to a village (Shawnee) on the Scioto river.

52. Possibly Wheeling Creek.

53. Muskingum River at Marietta, Ohio.

54. Kanawha River.

55. Cherokees.

56. This is probably an error in transcription and should read Niverville.

57. Refers to the Chickasaw War of 1739. A Canadian expedition was led by Charles Le Moyne de Longueuil (2nd Baron de Longueuil), 1687-1755.

58. The tribes that dwelt in present-day Illinois, the Kaskaskia, Cahokia, Peoria, Tamaroa, and Michigamea.

59. Fort de Chartres (at present-day Prairie du Rocher, Illinois).

60. Possibly the Little Miami River.

61. Pierre-Joseph Celoron de Blainville, 1726-1801.

62. This village was Pickawillany, a large English trading center, populated and administered by a mix of Indian nations. The foremost leader was La Demoiselle, called Old Britain by the English. This village was successfully attacked in 1752 by Charles Langlade and a party of Indians from Michigan (mostly Ottawas) and Old Britain was killed.

63. Charles (Chevalier de) Raymond, 1700-1774. He was born in France and came to Canada as an ensign in the colonial troops in 1722. Fort Miamis was at present-day Fort Wayne, Indiana.

64. Miami River.

65. Jacques Francois Le Gardeur de Croisille de Courtemanche, 1710-1777.

66. Francois Marie Bissot de Vincennes, 1700- 1736, was an officer of colonial troops who built a fort at the site of the Indiana town that bears his name. He was captured and burned in the Chickasaw expedition of 1736. Although it is possible that the remains of Francois were eventually brought north for burial it is also possible that this reference is to his uncle, Jean Baptiste Bissot de Vincennes, 1688-1719, who was a French representative with the Miami nation.

67. Detroit River.

68. Maumee River that enters Lake Erie at Toledo, Ohio.

69. Joseph-Pierre Bonnecamps, 1707-1790, arrived in Quebec in 1742 and taught at the Jesuit College. He returned to France in 1759. Although Celoron lists Father Bonnecamps as the Chaplain of the expedition his duties known (or unknown) to the Captain were probably more extensive. He was obviously a skilled scientist and this would account for his interest in accompanying Celoron. Also, the Jesuits were aggressive in their missionary efforts, often in competition with other orders. This was an excellent opportunity to capture a new territory. It must be noted that Jesuits did not normally serve as chaplains to the colonial troops. This was the duty of the Recollets (Recollects).

70. This report was prepared for La Galissonière.

71. An arpent equals .845 acres. It is also a measurement of distance, approximately 192 feet.

72. Fort Frontenac.

73. Measurement of distance, approximately six feet.

74. A bastion is a work that extends outward from the fort's wall (curtain) that allows the defenders to protect the face of the wall.

75. A demilune is an outerwork of a fortification. The placement here would protect the gate from direct assault or close-range artillery fire.

76. Now called the "French Castle," the building still stands at Fort Niagara State Park, Youngstown, New York.

77. Niagara River.

78. The British maintained a fort on Lake Ontario at the mouth of the Oswego River. It was established to entice some Fur trade away from the French. It also was a threat to the French line of communication with the west.

79. Wampum belts.

80. Probably Daniel Chabert de Joncaire. Chabert is used to avoid confusion with his older brother Philippe.

81. The Delaware Indian village of Kuskuski (present-day New Castle, Pennsylvania).

82. Buffalo.

83. Ottawas.

84. Perhaps a cadet. A Joannes was commissioned in the colony troops in 1759.

85. Fort Ponchartrain.

86. In practice, Detroit served as the regional supply and administrative center for posts and trade to the south and west. Fort Michilimackinac (Mackinaw City, Michigan) served in the same capacity for posts and trade to the west and north.

87. Fort St. Joseph at present-day Niles, Michigan.

88. Green Bay, Wisconsin.

89. Probably refers to the French post of Fort Ouiatenon on the upper Wabash River (near present-day West Lafayette, Indiana).

90. Approximately 600 feet by 200 feet.

91. On the north side of Lake Erie near Leamington, Ontario.

92. On the portage to the Richelieu River south of Montreal.

BIBLOGRAPHY

Dictionary of Canadian Biography. Volume III. Toronto: University of Toronto Press 1974.

O'Callaghan, E.B. (Editor) Documents Relative to the Colonial History of the State of New York. Volumes VI, IX, & X. Albany 1855, 1858.

Ohio Arcaeological and Historical Society Publications. Volume XXIX 1920.

Shortt, Adam (Editor). Documents Relating to Canadian Currency, Exchange and Finance During the French Period. Volume II. New York: Burt Franklin 1925 (Reprint 1968).

Stevens, Sylvester K., and Donald H. Kent (Editors). Wilderness Chronicles of Northwestern Pennsylvania. Harrisburg: Pennsylvania Historical Commission 1941.

Thwaites, Reuben Gold (Editor). Collections of the State Historical Society of Wisconsin. Volume XVII. Madison 1906.

INDEX

97

.

www.ingramcontent.com/pod-product-compliance
Lightning Source LLC
LaVergne TN
LVHW021537080426
835509LV00019B/2686